voices
messages in gospel symbols

Voices messages in gospel symbols

MARY KATHLEEN GLAVICH, SND

TWENTY-THIRD PUBLICATIONS
Mystic, Connecticut

CREDITS

Page 77: *A Thousand Reasons for Living* by Dom Helder Camara © 1981 is used by permission of Fortress Press.

Scripture texts marked NAB are taken from *The New American Bible*, copyright © 1970, Confraternity of Christian Doctrine, Washington, D.C., and are used by permission of copyright owner. All rights reserved.

Unless otherwise noted, Scripture texts used elsewhere in this work are taken from *The Jerusalem Bible*, copyright © 1966, Darton, Longman and Todd, Ltd., and Doubleday & Company, Inc., and are used by permission of the publisher.

Twenty-Third Publications
P.O. Box 180
Mystic, CT 06355
(203) 536-2611

Library of Congress Catalog Card Number 87-50859
ISBN 0-89622-345-0

Cover designed by Kathy Michalove
Edited by Andrea Carey
Designed by William Baker

FOREWORD

After reading Sr. M. Kathleen Glavich's book, *Voices: Messages in Gospel Symbols*, I went to my writing file, where I found several reflections that described, to some extent, the backside of her delightful "patchwork quilt of reflections."

Flannery O'Connor, the brilliant author of fiction, wrote that "the writer operates at a peculiar crossroads where time and place and eternity somehow meet. His problem is to find that location." Sr. Kathleen's reflections position us at the crossroads of fifteen images (e.g., sycamore tree, wine, turtledoves, towel). From the north come the writers of Scripture (evangelists, Isaiah, Tobit) sharing their experience of revelation regarding these images; from the south come the fiction writers (Henry van Dyke, Nathaniel Hawthorne, Flannery O'Connor) with their sensitivity to experience; from the east we encounter the perspective of philosophers (Teilhard de Chardin, Thomas More), and from the west some theologians (Thomas Aquinas, Thomas Merton) add their interpretation to life's meaning and the patches that make up our own quilted lives.

Good writers are often noted for their extensive reading. The creative act is in seeing "the connections" among the many sources. *Voices* makes the connections between the insights of writers and the experiences of daily life, between universal principles and specific events of history, between the action of grace and intensive human struggle. Because those connections are made, we all see better and are enabled to live more deeply.

In his excellent book *Inner Companions*, Coleman McCarthy states, "Yet he [John Muir] rarely let a day pass that some word or thought was not jotted on an odd piece of pocket-crammed paper, stowaway thoughts traveling secretly between his soul and heart." Not everyone is able to observe with care, much less articulate, those thousands of stowaway thought that hustle back and forth between our hungering soul and our thirsting heart. Sr. Kathleen has arrested several for us in these reflections. She has also captured many that pass between the memory and the imagination, chambers within our souls and hearts that ground us in the past and draw us toward the future.

From the recesses of our scriptural tradition comes the image of Zacchaeus in the sycamore tree, whose soul was longing for so much more than wealth and status. From the heart comes the cry of the turtledove, pining and yearning for its mate. From the memory comes the towel of the Last Supper, providing an image that makes our discipleship one of service. From the imagination comes pouring forth a water jar, perfume, and abundant wine to slake our parched lives—stowaway thoughts set free and shared generously with all who want to listen.

In *The Human Journey*, a biography of Thomas Merton, Anthony Padovano gives one of the qualifications of a writer: "Writing is a vow of conversation rooted in years of silence. A writer who does not listen well never knows what to say. One enters the silence not to be alone but to learn how to speak." Perhaps writers, in a sense, resemble good secretaries: people who record well what they hear and see. Writers are observers and lovers of the great conversations that fill our world.

Voices is a work of a writer who listens to the hidden depths of images and records the conversations heard, the beauty seen. In an age of noise and frenzied activity, it is a delight to find someone who stopped by a snowy woods to enjoy the darkness of the winter's night and the sound of falling snow.

A final reflection on writing, by G.K. Chesterton: "I have written the book, and nothing on earth would induce me to read it." History would probably demonstrate that Chesterton was being facetious. *Voices* should be read by parents, subway commuters, teachers, pastors, bartenders, and yes, even the author. There is no way of exhausting the power and meaning of images. Because of this book, images have spoken to us once again.

Bishop Robert F. Morneau
De Pere, Wisconsin

CONTENTS

DEDICATION

To my mother,
who first taught me how to speak.

ACKNOWLEDGMENTS

I wish to thank Sr. Mary Joell Overman, S.N.D., Sr. Rita Mary Harwood, S.N.D., Sr. Melannie Svoboda, S.N.D., and the many other members of my community who encouraged me to speak through the written word. I am especially grateful to Sr. Mary Luke Arntz, S.N.D., for graciously reading the manuscript and making suggestions at short notice. I am also indebted to Sr. Mary Catherine Rennecker, S.N.D., who carefully typed and retyped the manuscript; to those at Twenty-Third Publications who saw the book through production; and to Bishop Richard Keating and Brother James Townsend, who allowed me to tell their stories.

INTRODUCTION

I said to the almond tree,
"Sister, speak to me of God."
And the almond tree blossomed.
—*Nikos Kazantzakis*

Creators are mirrored in their creations. A song reflects the composer; a painting, the artist; a book, the author. In the same way, the universe, the masterpiece of the supreme Creator, reveals God. Its variety, its intricacy, and its magnitude attest to God's wisdom and power. Every created thing is an epiphany, echoing some aspect of the divine Being.

To behold a snow-topped mountain, its massive rocky slopes jutting boldly into the sky, is to know God's majesty. To sit at the foot of a waterfall and watch its refreshing rush of water cascade into a clear, deep pool is to see God's purity. To stroll through woods of lovely ferns, mosses, and lofty trees is to be enveloped with the peace and serenity of God. The fragile daisy and its velvety white petals and bright yellow center tells of the Creator's gentleness, while the shimmering, iridescent rainbow arched across purple-gray clouds bespeaks his beauty. A newborn baby is evidence of God's tenderness. Fire is a reminder of the energy of God's love. A monkey shows God's sense of humor and a giraffe, his unpredictability.

The psalmist is attuned to the speechless voices of the universe. He sings of the stars *(Psalm 19:1-4):*

The heavens declare the glory of God,
the vault of heaven proclaims his handiwork;
day discourses of it to day,
night to night hands on the knowledge.
No utterance at all, no speech,
no sound that anyone can hear;

9

yet their voice goes out through all the earth
and their message to the ends of the world.

St. Gregory of Nazianzus states in a hymn:
All things proclaim you—
things that can speak, things that can not... .
All things breathe you a prayer,
a silent hymn of your own composing.

In the same tradition, St. Francis of Assisi, the lover of
nature, exclaims in his "Canticle of the Sun":
Praise be to Thee, my Lord, with all Thy creatures.
Especially to my brother sun
Who brings us the day and through him Thou dost bright-
ness give;
And beautiful is he and radiant with splendor great,
Of Thee, Most High, he speaks.

More recently, in the writings of the French theologian
and philosopher, Teilhard de Chardin, the notion of creation
manifesting the Creator is a mighty refrain, especially in *The
Divine Milieu*: "...the great mystery of Christianity is not ex-
actly the appearance, but the transparence, of God in the universe."
The universe resounds with the glory of God.

Things are important to us. Partly spiritual, partly material beings, we live and work out our destiny in the realm of
matter. How we use it and abuse it determines our eternity. We
are free to expend and ravage the material universe for our own
power and pleasure, or we can share it. We can let it go to ruin,
or we can show concern for it. We can regard the world as the
lucky result of a coincidental combination of chemicals eons ago,

or we can cherish it as the love-gift of a personal God who cares about us. The latter point of view opens for us the possibility of finding in material objects a source of prayer.

When the Word became flesh and lived with us among color, hardness, roughness, scent and warmth, the Son of God reveled in the things of earth, the handiwork of the Father. Jesus saw that they were good, so good that he redeemed them along with us at the price of his life. Furthermore, he assigned them prominent roles in the act of redemption. During his public life, Jesus used concrete objects to teach. His audiovisuals were the birds of the air, the bread the women baked, the Temple in Jerusalem, and the roadside fig tree. Today, from the dimension where he dwells, he reaches out in the sacraments and touches us with things: water, bread, wine, and oil. Matter has been christened by his presence.

In particular, objects associated with Christ in the gospels have much potential for stimulating meditation. Each chapter of this book is a patchwork quilt of reflections on one of these things. Some of the topics, like the manger and the crown of thorns, are familiar. Others, like the turtledoves and the water jar of the Samaritan woman, are obscure. All become meaningful when considered with faith and love; all convey messages about popular themes such as hospitality, co-creation, peace and justice, respect for life, and reconciliation.

May these pages and the inspiration of the Holy Spirit draw the reader to Scripture, to prayer and to Jesus, so that he or she, too, may proclaim the greatness of the Lord.

1

MANGER

She wrapped him in swaddling clothes, and laid him in a
manger because there was no room for them at the inn.

Luke 2:7-8

J esus could have been born at home in Nazareth and
placed in a wooden crib fashioned and carved by his carpenter-
father, Joseph. Instead, because he makes his appearance on
earth while his mother and father are en route, he has no suit-
able place to lay his head. This circumstance is prophetic, for
over thirty years later, as an itinerant preacher, he will claim,
"Foxes have holes and the birds of the air have nests, but the
Son of Man has nowhere to lay his head" *(Matthew 8:20)*.

A manger is a feeding trough for animals. The French word
manger means "to eat." In the stable where Joseph and Mary
are forced to stay, the manger serves as a makeshift crib for
their baby, the Redeemer. God's propensity for foreshadowing

comes into play here. Not only is Jesus, our Life-Giver, laid in a feeding place, but his birthplace is Bethlehem, a town whose name means "House of Bread." It is as though God goes out of his way to underline that he is Bread for the world.

Eating is as essential to life as breathing. Daily we refuel ourselves with food. Omitting meals for any length of time leaves us weak and malfunctioning. No wonder that we pray in the *Our Father*, "Give us this day our daily bread." We look to God for life. When Jesus spends his first hours in a manger, he indicates that he is our bread, our life. Without him we can't survive. Interestingly, D.T. Niles in *That They May Have Life* defines evangelization as "one beggar telling another where to find bread."

As Jesus' journey on earth begins with wood, so does it end—not with the warm, welcoming wood of the manger, but with the rough wood of the cross. This wood, too, is associated with bread. The Body of Jesus nailed to the cross makes efficacious his words of the preceding evening when he held bread in his hands and declared, "This is my Body." The cross is the wood through which he becomes our life.

As a good parent, God has always provided bread for his children. When the world faced a famine in Old Testament times, God raised up Joseph to store enough grain to feed all nations. Years later, as the Israelites trekked through the desert on the way to the Promised Land, again they faced starvation. Yahweh had compassion on them. Daily he rained down manna from heaven during their forty-year sojourn to Canaan.

In New Testament times, when Jesus held the crowd's rapt attention for hours and they grew hungry, he felt their need. He astounded them by multiplying bread in abundance. Jesus continues to feed the hungry through his church. One of the first decisions of his followers was to appoint deacons to oversee the distribution of food to the needy.

Today Jesus still nourishes us in the form of bread. Whenever we share in the eucharist, we are energized for our particular journey on earth. As really as he rested in the manger Christmas night, as really as he hung on the cross Good Friday, Jesus comes into us when we partake of the sacrament. He unites himself with us and we become like him. But becoming like him means we become bread for others.

To be bread for others is to have compassion on them in their hungers. Where someone hungers for attention, we are there to listen. Where someone hungers for affirmation, we are there to encourage and support. Where someone hungers for understanding and sympathy, we are there to give solace. Where someone hungers for justice, we are there to set things right. In the words of Caryll Houselander, "The ultimate miracle of Divine Love is this, that the life of the Risen Christ is given us to give to one another, through the daily bread of our human love."

Fed at the eucharistic feast, we find our desire to be bread is intensified. We long to bring life to others. That is why Mother Teresa of Calcutta can instruct her novices, "Let the people eat you up." That is why, in anticipation of being thrown to wild animals in the arena, St. Ignatius of Antioch, who loved the eucharist, could say of himself: "I am the wheat of Christ. May I be ground by the teeth of beasts to become the immaculate bread of Christ." It is only in the eucharist that we find the power, the wisdom, the courage, and the love to satisfy the hunger of the people around us.

The manger brings to mind hospitality. It receives the child when the inns are closed to him. The child grows up to become the greatest and most gracious host the world has known. Jesus is a hospitable person from the beginning to the end of his public life. At the outset of his ministry, two of John's disciples stay the afternoon at his house. Jesus also enjoys the hospitality of others, frequently visiting Lazarus and his sisters Martha and Mary, and even inviting himself to the house of Zacchaeus for dinner. He socializes with Pharisees, tax collectors, and sinners, and he chides Simon for failing to perform the courtesies due to a guest. After the resurrection, he cooks fish on the shore and serves his apostles breakfast.

Jesus befriends the outsiders. His doors are open to everyone: the poor, the lonely, foreigners, lepers, all those whom society ignores and scorns. He makes them feel welcomed and relaxed. He gives them back their dignity by loving them. He requires a like hospitality in us, his followers, revealing that we will be judged on the way we receive the hungry, the thirsty, the naked, the stranger, the sick, and the imprisoned. Jesus was all of these when he came into the world at Bethlehem. He was all of them when he left it. He is all of them today.

As a newborn babe, Jesus was hungry, thirsty, naked, and weakened from the ordeal of birth. He was a stranger in Bethlehem. His divinity was imprisoned in flesh. At Calvary, as a condemned man nailed to a cross, Jesus was hungry and thirsty from the loss of blood, and he was naked. He was weakened from the torture. He was a stranger and outcast in Jerusalem and had been imprisoned. Today he suffers in his brothers and sisters.

A Spanish story tells of a priest searching in antique shops for a large replica of the crucified Christ. He comes across a Christ-figure removed from the cross and broken. Half of one leg is missing, an arm is missing, and the face is no longer discernible. Yet, the priest is strangely attracted to and moved by the figure and he purchases it. That night he speaks to his broken Christ, asking, "Who did this to you? Is he still alive?" Jesus answers, "Quiet! Forget the one who did this to me. I have already pardoned him. What is the greater sin—to mutilate an image of wood, or to mutilate my image in the flesh? You grieve over a broken wooden image while stretching forth your hand to harm the living Christs who are your brothers and sisters." When the priest suggests having the disfigured Christ restored, the Lord replies, "No, when you see me broken, you will think of the many people oppressed, tortured, and broken. They are without arms because they have no possibility of work, without feet because so many paths are closed to them, without a face because their honor has been taken from them. Many Christians who show devotion to a beautiful Christ forget him in their suffering fellow men and women."

The story tells us that when we welcome the marginal people, we welcome Jesus. John Paul II enlightens us as to how to act toward them: "You must never be content to leave them just the crumbs from the feast. You must take of your substance and not just of your abundance in order to help them. And you must treat them like guests at your family table."

The way we treat guests is the way we should always treat one another. How do we treat guests? We accept them as they are and overlook their faults. We are solicitous for their needs. We are anxious that they feel at home with us. We are polite, put our best foot forward and are willing to go all out for them. We listen to them, laugh at their jokes, and do not take them for granted. Just as Christ refuses no one who comes to him, we Christians are to be universal in our hospitality. Then someday we will hear him say to us: "Welcome to my Father's house. I have prepared a mansion for you."

Most obviously the manger symbolizes poverty. God certainly could have planned a more plush setting for his entrance into the world. Somehow, though, the stable with its smells, its crude crib, its earthliness, and its simplicity is right. Jesus identifies with the poor and lowly. His mission is to bring the good news to the poor (*Luke 4:18*). Even now he is more often found in huts than in mansions. He more freely mingles with those who have small incomes and large generous hearts than with those whose millions are poured into glorifying themselves. In the end, wealth is worthless unless we give it away. Only then will we have room in our house for the King of the Poor.

The manger also teaches us to be open to new roles in life. For years before Jesus came, some tree had silently grown and yielded the wood that a craftsman shaped into a feeding trough. But then it is called to a new and sublime state. Mary or Joseph exercises creativity and the manger is converted into a crib for the Son of God. The baby it holds is also the result of a transformation (*Philippians 2:6-7*):

His state was divine,

yet he did not cling

to his equality with God

but emptied himself

to assume the condition of a slave,

and became as men are....

How willing are we to slough off our old, comfortable selves and allow God to change us and use us for new tasks? Resisting God's efforts to recreate us may mean missing the opportunity of a lifetime. Trusting enough in God's goodness and love to give him a free hand with our lives can lead to marvelous, unexpected things. When Mary's angelic visitor proposed to overturn her marriage plans and Mary responded "Yes," a world was saved. When the Holy Family departed from the stable, the manger became a common trough again. It was needed to feed the animals. But thanks to St. Francis, who initiated the custom of setting up the creche at Christmas, the shining moment of the manger is remembered each year.

2

GOLD

Then, opening their treasures, they offered him gifts of gold and frankincense and myrrh. *Matthew 2:11*

First among the three gifts the kings from the east present to Jesus is gold. Gold is the best they can offer. This most precious metal is a gift for a king, fitting tribute to the newborn baby who is king of heaven and earth.

The infant is himself God's gift to us—the Son, the Father's treasure, not only a precious gift, but priceless (though he would someday be valued at only thirty pieces of silver). And this unparalleled gift is the culmination of a world full of golden gifts: sunbeams, dandelions, autumn leaves, golden agers and smiles. God is never outdone when it comes to gift-giving.

And what gift can we personally make in return? We would offer our all. Of ourselves this "all" might not amount to much. But the power of Jesus enables us to turn the dross of our daily lives into riches; Midas-like, we can change our moments into gold. This alchemy is achieved not by an incantation or a magic potion, but by intention. If we deliberately unite ourselves with Christ and our acts with his saving acts, our lives have consequences of cosmic proportions: they redeem humankind and give praise and glory to God. Furthermore, in surrendering ourselves to God, we become the possession of the Infinite One, and therefore our most mundane, insignificant actions take on untold value.

How good it is to desire to be pure, unalloyed gold, no atoms of us withheld from God and reserved for egotistical purposes or for idols. To make this desire a reality, we should not fear to be tested by fire. We can accept the pains of misunderstanding, persecution, physical or mental illness, the suffering of loved ones, all as somehow essential to our ultimate formation in the furnace of God's love. There, refined by this consuming love, purified and strengthened, we grow more worthy to be in God's holy presence for all eternity. Moreover, we take on the qualities of this divine love and flame it forth to others.

Gold is the most malleable and ductile of metals. Yielding easily to the artificer's touch, it is made useful and beautiful. Would that we were as docile in the hands of the Mastercraftsman. If every day we would heed God's voice urging us to pursue the good, if we would be open to the human instruments God uses to shape us, and if we would respond with trust and with hope to the events God allows to happen to us, then, to borrow Mother Teresa's words, we would truly make our lives something beautiful for God.

Unfortunately for us, instead of being co-creators, we sometimes thwart God's designs. Where we are challenged to choose the difficult, we respond with apathy or we flee. Where we are asked for mercy and understanding, we offer the cold rock of unforgiveness. Where we are invited to share the cross, we cry out in protest. Where we are expected to love and obey, we let pride and stubbornness rule us. And where we could make the time and space for God to work on us, we afford him only the leftover moments from our action-packed days. When we do these things, we are not true gold, but fool's gold.

The value of our lives is augmented only when we learn to listen, to let go, and to lean on God. To listen to God we have to tune in to God's many channels. God speaks in the still, secret depths of our hearts, stirring us to follow the nuances of his will. But we must be silent to hear. God doesn't shout to get our attention, but speaks to us through the good people placed in our path to direct us. But we must be open to them. God speaks to us in the inspired words of the Bible, but we must take it up and read it. God speaks to us in the church he promised to be with until the end of time. But we must not turn a deaf ear and let pride, prejudice, or fascination with modern trends block our obedience. To obey is to listen. And sometimes we hear what we don't like to hear.

We can listen to God in the rhythms of our life, the liturgy, and the seasons. We may have to strain our ears to discern him. We may have to listen with our heart, but when we manage to hear this "different Drummer," we perceive the music that gives meaning to life.

To let go is to drop our tight grasp on the reins of our life and let God be in charge. It means to give up our preconceived notions of God, ourselves, people, and things and let them be what they are. It means to stop playing tug-of-war when God tries to take something from us. It means to free ourselves from the strangling grip of compulsions. It means to retreat from the hectic, frantic race to do great things and to be a success, and just enjoy life for a while. It is to live in the now and not in the past or the future.

A story illustrates the difference. A man visiting a friend in Alaska decided to return home by car through the mountains. He traveled lonely roads that wound through scenes of unsurpassing beauty. Then the thought occurred to him that he hadn't seen a gas station for miles. Soon he became obsessed with the past and the future. At times he wished he were still back with his friends where he didn't have to worry about gas. At other times he longed for the future when he would be in civilization again where he could refill his gas tank. Eventually he reached his destination with gas to spare. There, when someone asked how he had enjoyed the scenery, he realized that most of the breathtaking landscape had been lost on him. He had not been able to respond to it.

The past and the future are unreal. They do not exist. To prefer them to the present is to cling to shadow instead of substance. It is to deny ourselves something wonderful. For each moment is an unrepeatable miracle.

To lean on God is to turn to him for strength and support. God invites us to come to him when we are weary and when we are in need. Not to draw on God's power when it is so accessible would be absurd. A woman terrified of her coming heart surgery receives the eucharist in the hospital and is flooded with the peace of Jesus. She faces the operation with courage and resignation. A priest at a poor inner-city parish, agonizing over a large bill, puts his problem in the hands of the Sacred Heart and receives a check from an anonymous donor for the exact amount of the bill. Whenever we are faced with a situation that calls for superhuman gifts, we can rely on God's friendship and love for our needs to be supplied. All we have to do is ask and God is there. The Spirit dwelling within us since baptism waits to be helper, consoler, and counselor.

Gold has always held a special allure. People have rushed to the ends of the world for it, slaved for it, married for it, fought for it, and even killed for it. For what? The most valuable things in life gold can't buy: faith, love, peace, wisdom, and grace, to mention a few. Gold's purchasing power is limited to influence and luxury. It doesn't guarantee happiness. In fact, it breeds anxiety, distrust, pride, and greed. Wealth is so conducive to corruption that our Lord resorts to a preposterous comparison and states that it is easier for a camel to pass through the eye of a needle than it is for a rich person to enter the kingdom of God.

Jesus also tells the story of a man who had so much grain that he instructed his men to build larger silos. That night the wealthy man died. His grain was of no use to him. When God judges him, God will not ask, "How many silos of grain did you collect?" but rather "When I was hungry, did you feed me?" Our treasure is not the material goods we accumulate in our lifetime, but the good we do for our fellow men and women. Our ambition should be not to own a vault of gold, but a heart of gold.

The Christian life is a paradox: we can give away everything and still be rich. Once we divest ourselves of the possessions that separate us from God and others, and smother our desire for them, the tapestry of our lives will be shot through with the golden threads of goodness, peace, and joy.

To discover gold is no easy task. Usually it lies buried deep in the earth and to mine it costs energy. Even if gold runs through streams on the surface of the earth, panning for it requires patience. To look for the gold in other people also takes energy and patience. In some people gold is hidden under a thick, crusty exterior. Only the eyes of love and faith are able to pierce their facade and search out their assets. Perseverance is usually rewarded. Once we find the qualities that make our neighbors lovable and concentrate on these, their faults are not so annoying. We hope everyone else discovers and appreciates the lode of gold in us to the point that our flaws, too, recede into the background.

The kings were wise to present the King of the Universe with gold, considering its symbolism. Ordinarily it is an appropriate gift for a king. In a way, though, gold is not the right gift for this king. What do you suppose he did with it?

3

TURTLEDOVES

...they took him up to Jerusalem to present him to the Lord...and also to offer sacrifice, in accordance with what is said in the Law of the Lord, a pair of turtledoves or two young pigeons. Luke 2:22, 24

As part of the purification ritual of a mother, Jewish law called for the sacrifice of a lamb and a turtledove or young pigeon. If the family couldn't afford a lamb, they could offer two birds. The poverty of the Holy Family again is brought into relief.

What kind of creatures are these birds who live only to die at the hand of the temple priest? They are as simple and gentle as the poor people they serve. Not for them the majestic and often violent power of the eagle, the bossy shrillness of the bluejay, or the ornate brilliance of the peacock. Their beauty lies in their simplicity. One day Jesus will exhort his apostles to be "cunning as serpents and yet as harmless as doves" (*Matthew* 10:16).

Doves are simple in appearance. They are a single, soft color. They are simple in their mild manner. Even their song is plain and soothing. They have a message for us. Simplicity is a rare virtue in our highly complex, sophisticated world of technology. Too many people live in the fast lane, their days blocked out in meetings, their minds constantly clicking out ways to outwit the next person before they themselves are outwitted.

How refreshing to encounter people free of the encumbrances of masks, pseudo-knowledge, and busyness, people who are wholesome. Simple people have God alone for a lodestar. They are drawn toward God as their one necessity. They make decisions in the light of God's law and order their lives by God's will, all the time seeking to love and glorify their Creator. St. Julie Billiart compared a simple person to a sunflower which always faces the sun. One who lives with this single-minded focus on God is stripped of the clutter of frivolous, fruitless activity and the entanglements of duplicity. Simplicity makes one artless: a pure, unflawed crystal reflecting sheer goodness.

Nathaniel Hawthorne illustrates this phenomenon in the short story "The Great Stone Face." A village is overshadowed by a craggy mountain which has the features of a wise and gentle man. A young boy named Ernest learns that a holy man, whose face resembles that hewn in the mountain, will someday come to the village. The lad yearns for the prophet to come. His life is dominated by the face in stone. In its presence he works and plays; it absorbs his thoughts and haunts his dreams. Each time a personage comes who promises to be the awaited one, Ernest is disappointed. In the meantime Ernest does much good for his people. He is kind and helpful. Finally, he is an elderly man revered by the villagers, and the holy man has not yet appeared. One day a visiting poet sees Ernest speaking to the people and is struck by the beauty of his face. He declares, "Behold. Ernest is himself the likeness of the Great Stone Face!"

What can be simpler than the life of a bird? We even have an expression, "free as a bird." A bird's only occupation, other than flying, food-searching, mating, and nest-building, is singing. When a bird sings, it is doing what it was created to do. Its song renders praise to its Maker. Even the raucous caw of the crow is pleasing to God. When we take the gifts God has given us, no matter how bountiful or meager, and use them in keeping with our Maker's design, we, too, create harmony in the universe. Our actions become worship.

Jesus does not admonish birds for their simple, carefree existence. Rather he says, "Look at the birds in the sky. They do not sow or reap or gather into barns; yet your heavenly Father feeds them" (*Matthew 6:26*). We can afford to stop our consumerism and our fierce competition, which spawn little more than tension headaches and ulcers. Our God is a loving God, protecting and caring for us as a mother hen for her chicks—a funny simile to compare God to a fowl! We could say it even verges on the sacrilegious, if Jesus himself hadn't used it. The unusual description emphasizes the tender and maternal aspects of God's providence.

Birds are unique in their ability to fly. Not bound to earth like other creatures, they skim treetops, swoop over oceans and soar above mountaintops, while human beings look on in envy. An activity that closely resembles flying is praying. In his essay, "Self-Reliance," Emerson writes: "Prayer is the contemplation of the facts of life from the highest point of view." At any time we are free to rise from the world and enter the realm of the spiritual. From this height, we are able to view our world from a better perspective. Relationships fall into place, patterns of daily actions emerge, and the road ahead is seen more distinctly. Through prayer, we are able to affect the lives of people on the other side of the world or in our own home. Through prayer, we can mount to the very throne of God where we can sing our love and praise and be caressed by the Divine. Whether it be in the secrecy of our hearts in our room, or aloud in community with our brothers and sisters—the mode doesn't matter—for a few moments or for an hour, praying lifts us into the heavens.

Birds have long been symbols of life and love. This symbolism can be traced in Scripture. Genesis, the book of beginnings, opens with the image of the Spirit of God hovering like a bird over the dark waters and then causing the chaos to burst forth in light and life. Later, Noah dispatched a dove to see if the floodwaters had receded so life could begin anew.

In the Song of Songs (*2:11-12*) the turtledove is the harbinger of spring, the season of new life:

...winter is past,

the rains are over and gone.

The flowers appear on the earth. . . .

The cooing of the turtledove is heard in our land.

At that time the bridegroom addresses his beloved as "My dove, hiding in the clefts of the rock, in the coverts of the cliff" (*2:14*). Because turtledoves are usually seen in pairs and their cooing seems to express the tenderest love and devotion, they are natural symbols for love.

At the threshold of the new creation, the Spirit again appears as a bird. When Jesus was baptized at the River Jordan, "heaven opened and the Holy Spirit descended on him in bodily shape, like a dove" (*Luke 3:21-22*). The Spirit, who is the bond of love within the Trinity, elects to take the form of a dove for a theophany. With the dove's appearance, Jesus is sanctioned and commissioned to bring eternal life to a sin-racked world. He begins to teach that love leads to life. He gives us what George Basil Cardinal Hume refers to as "manufacturer's instructions" on how to be fully human: the law to love God and neighbor.

Today the dove is also the symbol of peace, a gift intimately related to love and life. The mission of Jesus was to make peace between the Creator and the created. His mission is our mission. Our simplicity, our prayer, our love, and our zest for life should so animate us that we make peace happen in whatever spheres we find ourselves. If we are peaceful people, the calm, soothing strength of our presence will be balm for the wounded, the hurting, and the oppressed. We will conquer the bitter, the vengeful, and the aggressive not by the cold arms of conflict and power, but by healing arms outstretched to love and to help...by the arms of the Crucified.

The turtledoves of old laid down their lives for the poor. They probably did it singing.

4

WINE

...the steward tasted the water, and it had turned into wine. *John 2:9*

Wine holds the distinguished position in history of being the subject of Jesus' first public miracle. The setting is a wedding feast. Some might prefer a more solemn subject and backdrop for the debut of the Messiah. And they might wish for a motive with a life-and-death urgency. Instead, Jesus works the miracle to spare a young couple and their families social embarrassment. Furthermore, he does it at his mother's prompting, not on his own initiative.

Actually the circumstances are ideal. Wine and wedding feast. Both concepts evoke thoughts of celebration, exuberance, intoxication...and fullness of life. Both call to mind the kingdom of God. Wine is a sign of the new kingdom. The prophet Amos foretells the time of restoration in terms of wine. He says the days are coming "when the mountains will run with new wine and the hills all flow with it" (9:13). At Cana, Jesus changes 180 gallons of colorless water into excellent wine. John notes it was the third day—a resurrection strain. The new age has dawned. In our Lord's parables, wedding feasts are a symbol of heaven. That the first miracle occurs at a wedding feast signals the coming of the heavenly kingdom.

As for the motive of the miracle, the kingdom's hallmark is love. What better reason to work the first miracle than out of concern for one's neighbor and in deference to one's mother?

Wine is a time-honored ingredient of human celebration. By attending the wedding festivities and by supplying the wine, Jesus declares that celebration is good. His is the religion of lightheartedness. He banishes long faces, gloom, despair, and gnashing of teeth to the region of darkness and evil where they belong. He assures us that we have a loving Father, so we need not fret over food and clothing. He promises to be with us so that we can brave the troubles and suffering of life with confidence. He dies, so that we are free from the shackles of sin. He wins eternal life for us, so we can even laugh in the face of death. As God's people, we have much cause for celebration.

Having a good time is not inconsistent with the Christian lifestyle. No doubt the Father smiles to see his children thoroughly enjoying his gifts and one another's company. Ordinarily, we don't celebrate with enemies. In celebrating together we manifest our love. Laughing, singing, dancing, playing, and eating together not only expresses, but also strengthens, the bonds among us.

It's been noted that nowhere do the gospels record that Jesus laughed. A simple explanation is that the evangelists probably didn't bother to state the obvious. If Jesus was truly human, he certainly laughed at the wedding feast. Other situations, too, must have provoked a hearty laugh. How could Jesus keep a straight face when the children of Palestine gamboled around him, when Zacchaeus scrambled down from the sycamore, and when Peter gaped with astonishment on finding his tax money in a fish?

Jesus probably laughed from sheer delight at the happiness of Jairus and his wife when their daughter was restored, at the shy gratitude of the woman who was cured by touching his cloak, and at the discomfort-turned-excitement of the Samaritan woman at the well.

True, Jesus was a man of sorrow, acquainted with suffering; but he was also a man of joy who knew how to celebrate. He knew the heights of joy as well as the depths of sorrow.

Paradoxically, sorrow can give birth to joy. The grapes of the wine must be crushed before they yield sparkling wine. In life, it is the trials and pain that mellow and mature us. Joy is all the sweeter for the sadness that precedes it. Consider the crucifixion and the resurrection. To return to life is marvelous indeed. But to return to life after a humiliating and agonizing execution as a criminal is stupendous. When we have surrendered ourselves to the winepress and have suffered—especially when we have undergone persecution for justice's sake—then we are of more value to other people. We are more sympathetic, understanding, wise, and loving. The success of support groups is due to the shared wisdom of people who have suffered. The wine of our life can dull the pain of others and make them happy. It can bring them life.

Good wine is aged. How we despise waiting. We crave immediate results. In God's plan, though, many fine things develop slowly—canyons, trees, and diamonds. Eons passed before human beings appeared on earth and thousands of years more before we were redeemed. It seems to take forever to grow from adolescence to adulthood and to experience the healing of emotional wounds. The God-man too needed time to mature. Jesus let thirty years slip by before he began his public ministry. He demurred even as he worked the miracle of Cana, saying his hour had not yet come.

In Ecclesiastes 3:1 we read, "There is a season for everything, a time for every occupation under heaven." The secret is to discern the right times. If we rush headlong into decisions and changes without sufficient reflection and prayer, we may have to retrace our steps. Acting with precipitant haste can lead to disaster. The sage Aesop makes this the moral of the fable of the tortoise and the hare. The slow, steady tortoise wins the race, not the speedy hare.

Patience is a fruit of the Spirit—patience with God, with the church, with self, and with others. Often restless and discontented, we ask, "Why doesn't God straighten out the church—maybe by ending the turmoil by a public appearance—the Second Coming? Why doesn't God answer my prayers? Why do I make so little progress in eliminating pride, anger, or greed from my life? Why doesn't the church or my pastor get with it? Why are the people I live with moody and inconsiderate?" Like the infinitely patient God, we must wait.

The wine that Jesus produced at Cana was abundant and of superior quality. This extravagance is typical of God. Earth teems with a wild assortment of plants and animals. There is beauty and greatness where no person ever sees them, deep in our forests and oceans. Lovely flowers bloom and die in the woods unnoticed. Magnificent creatures swim where we have never gone. God is also radical in the way he shows his love. Jesus could have saved us by crooking his little finger, but he died an excruciating death. He goes to an extreme in order to remain with us. He becomes bread and wine that we may consume him. Always we can expect God to "do immeasurably more than we ask or imagine" (*Ephesians 3:20* NAB).

Jesus used wine in a comparison. He warned us not to put new wine into old wineskins. The mysteries of the new covenant were too grand to fit the structures of religion and civilization as they were known. The familiar, rigid categories of old thinking cannot contain the flood of the new, divinized life Jesus introduced. It bursts forth as surprisingly and irrationally as wine made from water. If we do whatever Jesus tells us, we too can drink the heady wine of the children of God. It will mean abandoning some of the notions, habits, and structures to which we've grown accustomed. It will mean trusting Jesus. It will mean letting the ever-creative Spirit guide us through the unforeseeable, uncharted future.

Our fear of new things is somewhat allayed when we reflect on history. Throughout the span of humankind's existence, it is change that has made us grow. Without change, we would never improve. We would still be cave dwellers clad in animal skins. From revolution to revolution, from Reformation to Counter Reformation to Vatican II, from the first to the third wave of Toffler, God has been our guide as he was for the Hebrews in the guise of a cloud by day and a pillar of fire by night. God has seen us collectively and individually through all the "future shocks" of the past. He has never deserted us, and we have endured.

Over and over God sustains us with miracles, those we recognize and those we do not. Gregory the Great wrote, "All wonder to see water turned into wine. Every day the earth's moisture, being drawn into the root of a vine, is turned by the grape into wine, and no one wonders." Not content with ordinary miracles, God performs extraordinary miracles on our behalf.

The same powerful and concerned one who turned water into wine, turned wine into his blood at his last banquet on earth. He has made this miracle present for the past two thousand years. Each time we share the cup, we commemorate Christ's surrender to death out of love. With each eucharist we are a step closer to that heavenly banquet where the choicest wine—life, joy, and peace—will never run out.

5

NETS

And they left their nets at once and followed him. Matthew
4:20

Peter and Andrew were casting their nets into the lake
when Jesus invited them to follow him and become fishers of
people. James and John were in their boat mending nets when he
called them. All four were netted by Christ that day. Ensnared
by his charm and the force of his message, they gave their
lives to Jesus—three of them to the point of death. What was it
that drew people to Jesus so strongly that they left their jobs,
their parents and families, their possessions and worldly ambi-
tions to follow him? The same magnetism today attracts people
who have never laid eyes on him. The simple explanation is
that he is the epitome of all we crave as human beings: truth,
goodness, life, and love.

Jesus alone can say, "I am the truth." He offers us reality, the meaning behind all mysteries. We can trust his words. There is no deceit in him. His teachings are true. His appraisal of us is true. He confronts us with truth and, like the Samaritan woman at the well, we are spellbound.

Jesus is sheer goodness. All his actions are full of grace. He spends himself doing good and inspiring others to do good. He heals the sick, casts out demons, and converts sinners—at personal cost. His compassion, his concern, his forgiveness are facets of his goodness. He is God, the all-holy One, with a face.

Jesus is life. As we grow older, life becomes more precious. How wonderful it is to fill our lungs with fresh air, to stand overlooking a lake with sunlight reflected on its waves, to listen to Chopin, to make a baby laugh, to embrace a loved one. Our whole being rebels against the thought of life ending. We want to live. Jesus makes eternal life possible. He promises that we will be with him forever. And he rises from the dead to give credibility to his promise. We who follow him on earth will follow him into the halls of everlasting glory. Then we will live and move and have our being in him forever and ever and ever.

Finally, Jesus is love. Everyone needs love, no matter how old or how self-sufficient that person may be. If we're deprived of love as a child, we grow up warped. If we feel abandoned by our friends, we become depressed. When we lack human love, we try to comfort ourselves with the devotion of our dog or parakeet. In Jesus we have the steady, unfailing support of divine love. When others would forsake us, grow tired of us, give up on us, he engulfs us with his tender love. His love is perfect: unconditional and undying.

To follow Jesus without compromise, we must leave our nets behind. We have to discard our net of greed, the drive to amass more and more for ourselves, because he is a poor one, who gives away what he does have. We have to shake free from the mesh of duplicity. Not for us the conniving of shrewd minds, a cutthroat existence. We are to live with the innocent simplicity of a child. Most importantly, we are to reject the snares of Satan, making deliberate, forceful efforts to rid ourselves of any hold he may have over us: in our bitterness, conceit, jealousy, or prejudices. As St. John of the Cross wrote, "A bird is restrained from flying by a thread just as well as by a strong cord."

We are to be perfect as our heavenly Father is perfect. But with confidence we can pray with the psalmist, "My eyes are always on Yahweh, for he releases my feet from the net" (*Psalm 25:15*). Alone we cannot untangle ourselves. But with God, nothing is impossible.

Nets are security, a means of livelihood. Jesus asks us to leave them to go where he leads, where things are insecure. A true disciple of Jesus does not have a comfortable existence. This is evident when we read the gospels. If we take to heart the beatitudes and the criteria for Judgment Day, if we look at the Master, we know that Christianity is not just listening to religious tapes in the privacy of a well-furnished room. It is not just celebrating a beautiful eucharist and avoiding serious sin. It's getting out into the fray of life and joining in the redemption of the human race by healing, caring, suffering, sacrificing, crying, and being persecuted. Christianity is fatigue, frustration, tension, and uncertainty. When all is well or too comfortable, something must be wrong. We have to ask, "What am I not doing that I should be?"

If Christians have a hard life, Mary, the first and best disciple, is no exception. One of her most well-deserved titles is Mother of Sorrows. Mary's unique relationship to the man of sorrows and her unwavering faithfulness to hearing the word of God and keeping it set the stage for the fulfillment of Simeon's dire prophecy to her: "A sword will pierce your own soul too" (*Luke 2:35*).

When Mary agrees to participate in the redemption of the human race, she leaves behind the ordinary life of a Jewish woman and begins the way of the cross. Because of her mysterious pregnancy, she suffers the slurs and raised eyebrows of her neighbors and the bewilderment and pain of her beloved Joseph. She endures the indignities of being rejected by the innkeepers and of giving birth in a stable. Fear grips her heart when she learns that Herod is determined to kill her child, and again years later when her boy is missing for three days. Only a mother can understand Mary's pain as Jesus left her to lead his own life, her grief when people called him crazy, and her sadness at realizing that, unlike other women, she would not have grandchildren. But can anyone fathom what Mary went through from the time she heard of Jesus' arrest until the next day when the body of her son was buried?

Mary's discipleship makes her not only a sufferer but a minister. She ministers to her elderly relative, Elizabeth, when both of them are expecting a child. At a wedding feast in Cana when the wine runs out, she does something about it. Then after Calvary, she cares for John and the other apostles. In short, Mary is our model in discipleship through her redemptive suffering and her ministry. She became a disciple by casting aside her own plans and dreams in answer to God's invitation to assist in carrying out the master plan.

Once free of our nets, we, like the apostles and Mary, are ready for a new career: we can be fishers of men and women. We can stride down the streets of this world in step with the Lord, healing, saving, loving. And how do we catch people for Jesus? We lure them with the same bait Jesus offered: truth, goodness, life, and love. When people see these qualities in us, they are naturally attracted. With the Holy Spirit, our invisible partner, working with us, how often a word or an action of ours is engraved on the minds and hearts of our children, co-workers, neighbors, or total strangers. Sometimes, years later, we discover the influence we had on them. Saints who have died hundreds of years ago, like St. Francis of Assisi, are still turning people to God. To proclaim the truth, to radiate goodness, to be full of life and hope, and to emanate love—that is our calling, that is our challenge.

For what have we traded our nets? A clear conscience, unbounded joy, and eventually piercing-sweet union with God.

6

PERFUME

*...a woman came in with an alabaster jar of very costly oint-
ment, pure nard. She broke the jar and poured the ointment on his head. Mark 14:3*

Every gospel relates the story of a woman who anoints
Jesus with perfume. In Matthew's and Mark's accounts, she is
just an anonymous woman in Bethany who pours the perfume on
Jesus' head. In Luke, she is a sinful woman whose tears fall on
his feet. She dries his feet with her hair and then pours perfume on them. In John, Jesus is at a dinner with Lazarus and
Martha when Mary pours the perfume on his feet and dries
them with her hair. Depending on the version read, the shock
value of the deed is augmented by the facts that the lady
crashed the party, she shattered the alabaster jar in the process of anointing, her hair was loose as no respectable Jewish
woman would have it, and the perfume was very expensive.

The dramatic impact of the extravagant gesture has not been forgotten. As Jesus predicted, "Whenever in all the world this Good News is proclaimed, what she has done will be told also, in remembrance of her" (*Matthew 26:13*).

Onlookers resented the waste of the precious ointment. If it had been presented as a gift, they reasoned, Jesus could have sold it and used the money for other things. Instead, the perfume was consumed to the last drop in one brilliant moment.

The anointing was a lavish act of love. People in love with other human beings are capable of seemingly insane actions. They do not care what others think. They sacrifice anything for the sake of their beloved. O. Henry's short story "The Gift of the Magi" illustrates this truth poignantly. Della and Jim are a young couple struggling to make ends meet. Della's prized possession is her long hair; Jim's is his gold watch. At Christmas time Della sells her hair to obtain enough money to buy Jim a watch fob, only to learn that Jim has sold his watch to purchase her a set of combs for her hair.

How much more unreasonable are those who are in love with God. They are willing to pour out themselves for his sake. Oblivious to the amazement, criticism, or denunciation of others, they live as they must in order to be united with the One who is everything to them. Their attitude is not "What do I have to do?" but "What more can I do?"

Love-gifts are never wasted. Ask a contemplative who has sacrificed a promising career for a life consecrated to God. Giving joy to the Beloved is worth any price.

Sometimes what appears wasted is ultimately very beneficial. When time and money are poured into a project that fails, when efforts to aid a troubled person yield no results, when overtures of love are spurned, then we can trust that in the divine economy a good has been achieved. And goodness, like beauty, is its own excuse for being. The shattering of the alabaster jar and the spilling of every drop of perfume was not in vain. Jesus claimed it served as an anointing for the time when his lifeblood would be poured out for love...another startling extravagance.

The fragrance of perfume filled the house. Invisibly and swiftly it permeated the air and touched all who were present, clinging to them and making them bearers of its loveliness. One of John Henry Newman's prayers begins, "Dear Jesus, help me to spread thy fragrance everywhere I go." The fragrance of Jesus. If we bring to others the sweet, fresh scent of integrity, purity, and divine love, it will change them and brighten their lives. The odor of sanctity is strong enough to drive out the stench of evil. But it is a mistake to equate it solely with the odor of incense, scented candles, and antiseptic. The smell of holiness is like the smell of bread baking, newly mown grass, and honest sweat. It's the smell of life, not death.

Good smells are pleasing to us. Women dab on perfume and men splash on cologne and aftershave lotion with a distinctive scent to make themselves more attractive. In designing the world, our provident Creator invented myriad flowers that are beautiful not only in appearance, but in their fragrance. He also saw to it that the aroma of food would enhance the delight of eating it. Praise God for the sense of smell.

The woman was right to anoint Jesus. "Christ" means the anointed one. The Hebrews anointed their kings, priests, and prophets with oil. The ritual of anointing consecrated them for their special tasks. Jesus was the Christ anointed by the Spirit to redeem the world. He filled all three roles: king, priest, and prophet. Just as the woman poured out her love for Jesus with perfume, he shows his love for us in anointing us with sweet-smelling chrism at baptism and again at confirmation. By our anointing we participate in his kingly, priestly, and prophetic missions.

Jesus is Lord and king. On Calvary the inscription over his head, "Jesus the Nazarene, King of the Jews," was a true epitaph, but too limited. Jesus is king of the universe. When the Father spoke the Word that brought all things into being, the Son was with him. When creation was held captive and tyrannized by the dominion of Satan, Jesus wrested it back by his death and resurrection. The Book of Revelation describes him riding a white horse: "On his cloak and on his thigh there was a name written: The King of kings and the Lord of lords" (19:16). His kingdom prevails over the kingdom of evil.

Through the sacraments of initiation, we become Christians, anointed ones. We are consecrated and become royalty: sons and daughters of God and heirs to the kingdom of heaven. We are consecrated to the spread of the kingdom of peace, justice, and love. We engage in the war against evil. Our motto: "To know him is to live; to serve him is to reign."

Jesus is priest. The Letter to the Hebrews explains how far his priesthood surpasses the priesthood of old. The sacrifice of Jesus is superior to the holocaust of animals. It is infinitely pleasing to the Father. Jesus himself is leader of the people. He leads in service, teaching through his life of compassion and concern.

We are a priestly people. The Jewish people saw themselves as priests. During their celebration of Sukkot, they offered seventy-two sacrifices, one for each known nation of the world. We, too, intercede for others as we pray the general intercessions, the Prayers of the Faithful, at Mass. Then through the eucharist we offer Jesus to the Father, the perfect sacrifice that has replaced all others. We also offer ourselves and hope that we, too, are sweet-smelling holocausts. We hope that by following the example of our High Priest we influence others, using our charism to lead all people to the Father. Our prayers, our deeds of love, our Christian bearing make us ministers to the needs of the world.

Jesus is prophet. He reveals God to us and proclaims what God desires of us. He calls us to live up to our covenant. As other Hebrew prophets were, he was ignored, mocked, despised, and eventually killed. His life and death were symbols of his message: God is love.

Our anointing consecrates us as prophets. We witness to Jesus, see reality as he sees it, and live according to his counter-culture values. Not surprisingly, we experience the same reactions he did: apathy, scorn, hatred. A bishop leads his people in a nonviolent attack on pornography and is criticized by the city's newspaper. A woman refuses to cooperate with the illegal practices of her boss and is fired. Undaunted, we go on, relying on the power of the Spirit of Jesus.

The woman's anointing of Jesus was a prelude to his death. At baptism Jesus anoints us, too, for our death. He enables us to live dead to sin in this life. In the end we will share his victory over death when we are raised to new and eternal life. Then, according to the revelations of Julian of Norwich, God will thank us for our service. And God's thanks will be so great that we will be filled with bliss. Then we will truly know the meaning of love.

7

FRINGE

And whenever he went, to village, or town, or farm, they laid down the sick in the open spaces, begging him to let them touch even the fringe of his cloak. *Mark 6:56*

The fringe of Jesus' cloak was the tassel that the observant Jew wore at each corner of his garment. Even this fringe emanated power. Touching it brought healing. Many trifles in the universe could be compared to the fringe of Jesus' cloak. They are seemingly insignificant, perhaps only for decoration, but they are a means of coming in contact with him. As someone once said, God is in the details.

Buried in each of us is an intense yearning for God. We long to feel God's power surging through us to purify us of everything that is low. We want to be healed so that we can be the dignified, dynamic persons we were meant to be. In Greek mythology, Antaeus was a giant who was invincible as long as he touched the ground. His energy was ever renewed by contact with earth. Likewise, we must remain in contact with God, the ground of our being. In God we will have full life. We wish simply to be in God's presence and bask in his goodness and love. With the psalmist we pray (42:1):

As a doe longs
for running streams,
so longs my soul
for you, my God.

Our thirst can be quenched in some measure if we are sensitive to God in fringe-like things and happenings. The dew on the lawn, a kind word, a chance meeting with a friend, an unexpected raise are gifts from God. For those who have eyes of faith, nothing is profane. God's providence arranges the daily occurrences of our lives. Through them God communicates with us and shapes us into our best selves. Surrounded by evidences of God's love, we have only to reach out to find him.

Some days we will find God only through fringe. When the sky is overcast by dark clouds—hanging heavy and threatening—they sometimes part for a few seconds and radiant sunlight pours forth. Our life is often lightened like that. Nothing is right. We are overcome by lethargy. The world caves in on us. In our spiritual sickness, we long to grab hold of some divine fringe. Then some brief divine breakthrough is our saving factor. The form varies. We receive a long-awaited letter. We observe a toddler laughing with glee at the feel of a kitten's fur. We suddenly remember a time when God showed his concern for us in a striking way. These experiences sustain us to weather the storm.

Imagine the loss if on his way to Jairus' house, Jesus had refused to be interrupted by the woman who touched the fringe on his cloak. Sometimes graces come in the form of interruptions. We are engrossed in a pet project or concentrating on a job that has to be done. Then a friend drops in for a chat, the phone rings with someone requesting a minute of our time, or a tooth begins to throb. We dislike interruptions because they spoil our plans. Rather than becoming annoyed and frustrated, we can regard these nuisances as grace-gifts, the "fringe" benefits of our days.

This morning was a free day. An alarm rudely interrupted my sleep an hour before I intended to get up. My first impulse was anger. This prevented me from going back to sleep. Angry thoughts intruded into my morning prayers. However, I later enjoyed an extra hour of leisure time, doing what I like best. This particular interruption was ultimately good for me. So much of our happiness depends on our attitude, not only to interruptions, but to any circumstance. In the words of John Milton, "The mind is its own place, and in itself can make a heaven of hell, a hell of heaven."

What we perceive of God now is only fringe. Yes, Jesus revealed his love, and creation affords us a glimpse of his magnificence. But who God is, is far beyond our comprehension. Different religions have given God different names and faces. We make feeble attempts to grasp God by inferring what he is like from what we are like. We try to box God in, but he forever eludes us. For the reality of God surpasses human terms and concepts. God is always bigger, always more than, and totally "other" than, our words and thoughts.

Augustine likened our efforts to understand God to a boy on the beach running back and forth trying to put the ocean in his pail. The exercise is futile. Thomas Aquinas' writings were a peak achievement in intellectual history. Yet, in his wisdom Thomas recognized them for what they were in the light of God: straw.

Impelled by grace, we continue to pursue the divine because, as Thomas Merton writes in *Signs of Contradiction*, "Man goes beyond himself by reaching out toward God, and thus progresses beyond the limits imposed on him by created things, by space and time, by his own contingency."

A true knowledge of the vast distance between God and us would probably crush us. The only thing that saves us and gives us hope is another incomprehensible mystery: God exhibits a special love for us.

In every Christian circle some people are the fringe of the Mystical Body. They are not officers of organizations or headline makers. They quietly go about their work with great dedication but little recognition. Yet these people are as important as a pope. In fact, they are the ones who cement our parishes and communities together. Often the power of Jesus is exerted through these fringe-people, bringing strength and healing to others. Their very ordinariness makes them approachable and non-threatening. Their dependability brings projects to a successful conclusion.

The woman who counted on a cure by unobtrusively touching Jesus' cloak from behind was a person on the fringe herself. Her illness made her an outcast among her people. Yet, like every person, she was important to Jesus—important enough to stop for, to work a miracle for, and to redeem by the price of his blood.

One day my sister was in an accident on the freeway. She sat behind the wheel of her car staring in horror at the car she had plowed into. A truckload of hippies, unkempt and long haired, stopped and managed to get her out of the car. They sat with her on the curb while she waited for the police. Meanwhile, a man and his son were driving along the freeway. Spotting the group on the curb, the man remarked to his son, "Look at them. Serves them right." At that, he crashed into the back end of my sister's car. His collision not only taught him to keep his eyes on the road, but it opened his eyes to the fact that hippies, like any other people, can be good.

Sometimes the most unlikely people hold astonishing graces for us. But we'll never know that unless we come into contact with them and are open to receiving their gifts. How often, for instance, a family and friends experience God's love in a new way through a child with a handicap. Or how many people find their lives enriched by the friendship of an octogenarian or a prisoner on death row. When we seek out the people on the fringes, we never know what surprises the Lord has in store for us.

8

LEFTOVERS

They all ate as much as they wanted, and when the scraps remaining were collected they filled twelve baskets.

Luke 9:17

Why did Jesus furnish an overabundance of food when he multiplied the loaves and fish? Surely if he could number the hairs on our head, he could have calculated the exact amount needed to satisfy the hungry throng. His leftovers must hold a message for us.

Perhaps Jesus' generosity just could not be contained. This is in keeping with the pattern of divine actions. It would have been sufficient to make enough stars to fill our sky at night, but instead God created galaxies in the fathomless space beyond our sight. A few types of animals would do, but we are blessed with thousands of fascinating species. A small supply of sperm and eggs would be enough to continue the human race, but we each have many chances to bring forth new life. Our world could have been designed in plain black and white, but we enjoy it in color. To be prodigal is a habit with God.

That Jesus doesn't bother to count is obvious in his sacrifice. Not only does he offer himself to the Father for us on Calvary, but he makes his offering present again and again on our altars from one generation to the next. His forgiveness, too, is boundless for all who seek it. He is willing to forgive seventy times seven times—an infinite number of times—as he asks us to do. There are other ways he instructs his followers to imitate him—by being extremists in love. He says, "...if a man takes you to law and would have your tunic, let him take your cloak as well. And if anyone orders you to go one mile, go two miles with him" (*Matthew 5:40-41*). He preaches and practices the ultimate generosity: love of our enemies.

The lavishness of God's love is mirrored in Richard Pindell's short story "Somebody's Son." Against his parents' wishes, a young man decides not to go to college but to leave home and make his own way in the world. After a maturing experience as a grape picker, he realizes that the best course for him is to swallow his pride and return home. He writes a letter asking his dad to tie a yellow ribbon on a tree in the orchard if he is welcome back home. As the train the boy is on is about to pass his father's property, the boy panics. He asks the passenger next to him to look out the window and tell him if he sees a yellow ribbon on a tree. "Son," replies the man, "every tree in the orchard has a yellow ribbon."

Whereas the surplus bread and fish is possibly a sign of love, maybe the gathering of the scraps after the grandiose picnic is a sermon against littering. Mark comments that the groups seated on the grass looked like flowerbeds. Contrast this delightful picture with the scene afterward if the people had left the remnants of their meal strewn all over the ground.

What an eyesore! Yet, isn't this what so many of our cities and roads have become, a dumping ground? After Fourth of July fireworks, one town had to spend thousands of dollars to clean up the debris the crowd had left behind.

Without our interference, nature constructs gorgeous scenery characterized by cleanliness and purity. But we make a shambles of our environment. Beer cans, bottles, and paper containers spoil the beauty of our landscapes. Waste products pollute our oceans, lakes, and rivers. Before it is too late, more of us must take seriously our responsibility as stewards of creation. We ought to care for our earth-home with pride and gratitude. It is a gift for our enjoyment and for the enjoyment of future generations.

The collection of leftovers also teaches us not to waste. It could be that the scraps of bread and fish were sizeable portions that were saved to fill the stomachs of the poor of Palestine. In our relatively affluent society, we tend to dispose of things when they still have value, if not for us, then for someone else. It takes extra time, energy, and thought to make use of leftovers, to recycle goods, and to contact the St. Vincent de Paul Society. A creative person will find a use for anything. So will a conscientious steward.

The throwaway mentality that induces us to get rid of imperfect things and leftovers is stealthily affecting our approach to living things—including human beings. If an ultrasound test indicates that a baby in the womb is flawed, a mother can have her child aborted. If a driver has the gall or misfortune to cause an accident, the owner of a handgun can forestall future problems by eliminating the "crazy driver." If a sick or aged person is a burden to others, there are ways he or she can be disposed of. Hearing of such atrocities day after day dulls us to their horror. It's as though our nation's conscience were being anesthetized.

How do we reclaim a reverence for life? By coming to a better understanding of what life is. God reveals in Scripture that life is a gift. God created all living things and sustains them. In the Book of Job, Chapters 38 through 41, God asks Job in various ways, "Where were you when I brought forth creation?" This passage helps us see our relationship to the world in proper perspective. How do we "nothings" called into existence by the eternal and omnipotent One dare to harm what is his? We have no rights over one another. When we usurp them, we tread on dangerous ground.

Furthermore, each person is made in God's image and likeness and is precious. God loves every one as his child. He chose to suffer and die for our happiness. God wishes to live with each one forever. An attack on a human being is exceedingly offensive to God who treasures that person as the apple of his eye.

Life is an awesome mystery. We are still unlocking the secrets of its origin. We are astounded at the intricate laws that govern the competition, function, and instincts of living things. The brain, an eyelash, even a single cell are beyond our comprehension. No one has given himself or herself life. No one has brought another person to life. We are hardly in a position to judge that someone else's life is like a leftover, good for nothing.

If only everyone shared Carl Rogers' stance toward life. He said, "People are just as wonderful as sunsets if I can let them be. I don't try to control a sunset. I watch it with awe as it unfolds, and I like myself best when appreciating the unfolding of life."

To some people the gathering of leftovers may smack of perfectionism, a bad word today. In a reaction against the rigid perfectionism that once stifled life, perhaps we have unwittingly suppressed the values of excellence, professionalism, and "class." An old adage counsels that if we aim for the stars, we may reach the barn roof, but if we only aim for the roof, we may never get off the ground. Striving for all "tens" should not be confined to the Olympics. If we don't challenge ourselves to improve, we won't improve. However, we share the physical world's tendency to inertia. We are comfortable performing in a mediocre way. There's less stress. The easy way out may prolong our lives, but will it make us what we truly wish to be?

It would not be so bad to receive a scrap of a miracle. The Syro-Phoenician woman was content with that. Her daughter was cured after she pointed out that even the pups receive scraps from the table. A small piece of a miracle is better than none. Would that we had the wisdom to say, "It's a miracle that I don't get killed merging into highway traffic. It's a miracle when the dentist tells me I don't have any cavities. It's a miracle when in searching for something in a book, I immediately open it to the right page. It's a miracle that so many people have loved me in my lifetime."

Apparently each apostle customarily carried a basket with him on his travels. That there were twelve baskets is significant. There were twelve tribes of Israel and twelve apostles. The number twelve is the sacred number symbolic of the fullness and glory of the future kingdom. The odds and ends, the remnants of the meal, were gathered together by those Christ appointed. At the end of time the little ones, the anawim, also will be gathered into the kingdom and judged by them. In the Book of Revelation, these citizens of the new Israel total one hundred and forty-four thousand (12 x 12 x 1000). If we pay attention to leftovers, someday we may find ourselves among those sealed as servants of God.

9

SYCAMORES

[Zacchaeus] ran ahead and climbed a sycamore tree to
catch a glimpse of Jesus who was to pass that way.

Luke 19:4

Most people have favorite trees: the oak from which
Dad hung an old tire, the apple tree whose lowest branch is the
perfect perch for reading, the quiet willow by the side of the
stream. No doubt, Zacchaeus' favorite tree was the sycamore
that boosted him toward Christ and salvation.

How convenient for Zacchaeus that a sycamore tree grew
along Jesus' route. According to the *Jerome Biblical Commen-
tary*, a sycamore's short trunk and wide lateral branches make
it ideal for climbing. So Zacchaeus took advantage of what nature provided, a tree, to make up for what nature had denied
him, height. The wealthy tax collector, probably pompous and
rotund, clambered up the tree. He was not afraid to be up a tree
in order to see Jesus.

Keeping our eyes on Jesus is not easy. It requires initiative, courage, and discipline. Sometimes it means risking our job, our friends, our reputation, or our life. Sometimes it means standing alone. Followers of Jesus must be willing to be labeled "fool," "oddball," and "goody-goody" as well as "troublemaker." After all, "The disciple is not superior to his teacher..." (*Matthew 10:24*).

Archbishop Oscar Romero knew what it was like to be out on a limb for Jesus' sake. For three years he preached Christ's values of justice and peace, condemning the injustice and violence perpetrated by the government of El Salvador. He endured mockery and persecution. Four other bishops in his country opposed him. The church transmitter that broadcast his sermons was destroyed by a bomb. He was the object of a million-dollar smear campaign. Aware that he was on "the list," the Archbishop offered his blood for his people. He refused personal protection, saying, "The shepherd does not want security while security is not given to his flock." On March 25, 1980, Oscar Romero was gunned down as he celebrated Mass in the cancer hospital where he lived. His foolhardiness gained him the beatific vision.

Granted, we are not all called to be martyrs by blood. We all know, though, how daily decisions and circumstances can be calls to Christian heroism. We draw strength to answer these invitations from our union with Jesus through prayer and the sacraments, and from people who share our vision. When we encounter someone living simply or hear of someone forgiving an enemy, then we are more disposed to live that way ourselves. We are so interrelated in the body of Christ that we constantly affect one another. Our goodness and the good we do somehow influence everyone else. Unfortunately, so do our badness and the bad we do.

One way we can exert a positive influence is to play the sycamore tree in the lives of people searching for God. If we are deeply rooted in love and faith, we are able to offer others the support they need to behold the divine. A woman invites her friend to return to the church and accompanies her to the sacrament of reconciliation. A man lends a co-worker a good spiritual book. A busy pastor makes time to counsel a seventeen-year-old who is undergoing a crisis of faith. Evangelization is every Christian's mission. We carry it out by raising our children to faith, by participating in the parish CCD and RCIA programs, and by contributing to the missions at home and abroad. To lift others to Jesus we needn't proclaim him on street corners. Our lives shout him by our kindness, prayerfulness, and concern.

Trees figure largely in salvation history. Many of them are symbols of life. Genesis tells how God planted the tree of life in the garden. This same tree grows in the city of God described in the Book of Revelation. Jesus spoke about the kingdom of God in terms of a flourishing mustard tree in whose branches many birds nest. On the other hand, some biblical trees represent death: Eden's tree of the knowledge of good and evil, the tree that ensnared Absalom's hair, making him easy prey for the enemy, and the fig tree Jesus cursed for its lack of fruit. The tree of the cross paradoxically belongs to both categories. Although it is an instrument of death, it brings about eternal life.

Zacchaeus' tree is a symbol of life. It leads to reconciliation, a characteristic of growth. Sin saps our energy and results in decay. It is a disease that also harms those around us. Although sin is really not a black mark on our souls, it makes us feel dirty, marred. When Zacchaeus is healed and purified by Jesus, not only he, but everyone in his house and in the neighborhood benefit.

Jesus still works dramatic miracles of grace in some sinners. Jim Townsend served a sentence for killing his pregnant wife. She had tried to prevent him from attacking a man during a card game. While in prison, Jim came to know Jesus better and he was drawn to him. When he was released, he became a Franciscan brother. Now he is devoted to bringing other people to Jesus, the Life, by his preaching.

Undeniably, the healing of our body is remarkable. We scrape a knuckle. Soon a scab forms. Underneath, skin grows, just enough to fill the injured space. The scab shrinks and falls off, uncovering the new layer of skin. Gradually even the scar fades. Broken bones, too, knit to become whole again. Likewise, our supernatural life can be healed when it is damaged. Through the encounter with Christ in the sacraments, we are repeatedly restored to health. There our fractured humanity is mended by the divine Physician. The working of grace makes us like new.

It is always possible for a Christian to make a 180 degree turnabout to God. But such conversions are few. Today the concept of life-long conversion has taken hold. We realize that all of us are continually challenged to turn more toward the Lord. In many ways the Spirit is quietly renewing the earth. How appropriate that the Renew program, a program for continual conversion, has chosen a tree for its logo, a symbol of life and growth.

A major part of conversion involves being reconciled with one another. The all-too-human reaction to an offense or injury is to return evil for evil. The number of liability suits in recent years has skyrocketed so that liability insurance is practically unaffordable for most. The entertainment media advocate revenge along with their general sale of violence.

Contrary to today's culture, Jesus taught forgiveness. He lived it when he forgave his executioners as he was dying on the cross. His followers try to live it. The world was stunned at the sight of John Paul II embracing his would-be assassin. Actually, forgiving is healthy. Unforgiveness threatens our well being. Harbored within a person, bitterness snowballs until it destroys individuals, families, and nations.

Anyone who has borne resentment toward another knows how miserable it makes one's own life. To nurture a grudge, one must always be on guard, one's thoughts are absorbed, and sleep is lost. Like other evils, this hardheartedness is upsetting emotionally and perhaps even physically. If we would abolish all silent treatments, petty meannesses, retaliations, grudges, and lawsuits, much of our suffering would disappear.

But in order to be a peacemaker by extending forgiveness, we have to be strong. We have to own a good self-concept. Then we will be free enough to be humble and loving and Christian. We will be able to say "I forgive you." We will also be able to say "I'm sorry." With Jesus' loving encouragement, Zacchaeus could do both.

Trees are majestic creatures. Upheld by sturdy trunks, they reach into the sky and tower over us. Whether the wind rustles or howls through their branches, they only bend and sway. Psalm 1:3 makes an apt comparison. It says a just person "is like a tree that is planted by water streams, yielding its fruit in season, its leaves never fading." An upright person has an air of dignity. Moreover, he or she bears much good fruit.

Trees have multiple uses. They provide shade, fruit, lumber, tea, and maple syrup. We have seen how Zacchaeus' tree served both as a ladder to God and as a bridge to reconciliation with God and others. Shel Silverstein beautifully illustrates the concept of total sacrificial love by means of a tree. In his book, *The Giving Tree*, a boy receives gifts from his tree all his life long. At the conclusion of the story, the boy is an old man, and nothing is left on the self-sacrificing tree but a stump. Generous to the end, the tree invites the old man to rest on the stump.

We can imitate this self-giving by sharing with others our time, talents, and treasure. We truly give ourselves to others in the simple gift of presence. The sycamore tree was there when Zacchaeus needed it. Michel Quoist recounts a time when his presence meant a lot to a little stranger. One evening during a stay in the hospital, he heard sobbing. He traced the sound to a child who was severely burned. He sat beside the child a while and talked soothingly. Whenever he got up to leave, the child's crying increased. Quoist spent the rest of the night being there with the child, helpless to relieve the pain, but offering comfort nonetheless. It is important to be with others: in hospital rooms, at wakes, at graduations, and at celebrations. It is important to be waiting up for others when they come home. Our presence speaks volumes. Conversely, how lucky we are if we have friends who are reliable, who are there at the right time. "Grapple them to thy soul with hoops of steel," Shakespeare advises in *Hamlet*.

Trees, like the sycamore, raise our minds to God by their beauty. Palm trees, fir trees, giant redwoods, and a multiplicity of other trees enhance our planet. With the changing of the seasons, most trees advance from one kind of beauty to another. In the summer, luxuriant forms clothe the land with shades of green. In the fall, flaming leaves set the world afire with brilliant yellows, oranges, and reds. Winter days alternately bring breathtaking scenes of bare, black branches against purple skies, snowladen limbs, and ice-encased trees glistening with cool beauty. Then the coming of spring is heralded by a rush of light green buds and lovely blossoms. No wonder Joyce Kilmer in his poem "Trees" concludes, "Only God can make a tree."

Trees evoke images of play. Who has not built a treehouse, swung from vines, picnicked under a tree, or hidden his or her face against the trunk of a tree counting to a hundred for a game of hide-and-seek? To play is to be like the child Jesus exhorted us to resemble: carefree and ready to be thrilled by life. Anyone concerned about well-being attempts to balance work and play. Our bodies, minds, and souls need periods of relief from pressure and tension to be re-created. Once we are rejuvenated through play we can accomplish our work more efficiently and do it in a happier frame of mind.

Equally important, it is through play that we come to know ourselves and others better. We have time to reflect on who we are and what we're doing. Through playful interaction with others, we discover truths about ourselves, consoling as well as disturbing. We also forge the bonds of friendship and community more strongly through such experiences as the shared joy of viewing a funny movie together and the healthy competition of a good tennis match. On the whole, "One could do worse than be a swinger of birches," as Robert Frost comments in his poem "Birches."

Since Zacchaeus' time, tree climbing has become well established in Christian tradition. Taking on himself the sins of the world, Jesus climbed a tree to become the Great Reconciler.

10

WATER JAR

The woman then left her water jar and went off into the town. *John 4:28* NAB

As the Samaritan woman sets out to do her daily chore of drawing water, little does she suspect that her life will change drastically. At the well she meets an unusual man who violates the current cultural code on two counts. He, a man and a Jew, addresses her, a woman and a Samaritan, to ask for a drink. Jesus usually puts all protocol aside and gets to the heart of the matter. He proceeds to baffle her more by offering her living water, water that springs up as a fountain for eternal life. But he leaves her dumbfounded when he reveals knowledge of her multiple marriages. She concludes that he fills the qualifications of the promised Messiah. Her conjecture confirmed by Jesus, the woman becomes the first female evangelizer. She goes to tell her townspeople the good news. Either in her haste or as an answer to Jesus' original request, the woman leaves her water jar behind.

Water is not only central in the story of the woman at the well, but it is central to life in general and to Christian life in particular. Three-fourths of the world is water. Our own bodies are 70 percent water. Life depends on water. This was poignantly demonstrated when millions of Africans starved to death because of droughts. Water supplies energy to illumine our homes and run our computers. We use it for travel and for transportation. It offers us a wide range of recreational activities from floating to boating. It is the basic cleaner and the most common thirst quencher. With good reason St. Francis of Assisi prayed, "Praised be my Lord for sister water, which is greatly helpful and precious and pure."

Water, moreover, is a source of beauty in its many forms: oceans and ponds, powerful waterfalls and crooked little streams, gentle rains and torrential downpours, snowflakes, waves, and rainbows. As rain, it carves grand canyons; as trickles, it sculpts strange stalagtites and stalagmites; and as frost, it designs lacy patterns on window panes. No wonder water is such an eloquent symbol.

In the story of Helen Keller, water awakens the blind and deaf girl to the real world. When Helen suddenly connects cold water splashing from the pump with the word "water," she is plunged into life. Similarly, it is water that begins the Christian's story. In baptism, water floods us with supernatural life. It cleanses us, frees us, and strengthens us. We are born from water to a new life as sons and daughters of God.

According to the Hebrew Scriptures, God the Life-Giver likes to play with water. In Genesis, the Spirit hovers over the water and creation comes into being. Later, during Noah's time, God uses a deluge to purify the world and start it anew. In Exodus, God conducts the chosen people safely through the Red Sea to a new life of freedom. God has Moses sustain them in the desert with water from a rock.

Jesus himself is baptized, coming forth from the River Jordan anointed for a new life. He turns water to wine, calms angry waves, walks on water, and twice makes the Sea of Galilee yield a miraculous catch of fish. We can believe him when he offers himself as a drink: "If anyone thirsts, let him come to me; let him drink who believes in me" (*John 7:37-38*). This is what the Samaritan woman learns.

Flannery O'Connor presents the water-life theme effectively in her short story "The River." A small boy is only in the way in the apartment where he lives. His mother and father are more concerned with drinking with friends than in feeding him. When a babysitter takes him to a meeting at the river one day, he is baptized. There he matters. He is not a problem, but a person. In the end he chooses the river over the apartment. We are all confronted with the same decision: Do we choose life through death, or a living death? Jesus makes us important as he made the Samaritan woman important. He impels us to choose life, but he never compels us. He leaves us free to choose him.

Holy water, a sacramental, recalls our baptism. We bless ourselves with it as we enter and leave the church. Sometimes the eucharistic celebration opens with an asperges ritual in which the priest sprinkles all the people of God with water. Water is blessed as holy water during the Easter Vigil services. This is because the water used in baptism derives its special powers from the death and resurrection of Jesus. Ever since the Paschal mystery removed the sting of death and conquered sin, the waters of baptism, coupled with tears of repentance, extinguish the fires of hell for us.

Water is linked with divinity. Its transparency suggests the supernatural as does its power. Also, the awesome companions of rain, thunder, and lightning draw one's thoughts to God. In many times and places, miraculous powers have been attributed to water. For instance, the Ganges is sacred to the Hindus; the fountain of youth enticed Ponce de Leon to cross an ocean; and annually, thousands of pilgrims visit the healing waters of Lourdes. In addition, water exists in all three states: solid, liquid, and gas. For this reason Christians regard water as a symbol of the Trinity, like the three-leaf clover.

Saints and spiritual writers have even likened Jesus to a large expanse of water. The analogy is easily drawn. Jesus is our life. He is the medium in which we thrive. Apart from him we die, like a fish out of water. He buoys us up more than we realize. Jesus is the all-encompassing sea of peace, an ocean of love. To drown in him is to live.

Water is ordinary. It's served free of charge at restaurants. It flows at the flick of a wrist from any number of taps in our houses. Graces are just as available. How often do we contemplate the "ordinary" graces that come to us each day? A list could include the grace of getting out of bed to face a hard day, the grace of a friend's enlightening us about one of our faults, the grace to hold our tongue when we are tempted to devastate another person, the grace to do our best when we could get by with a slipshod job, and the grace to pray. Actually every person who comes across our path, every event is a grace-gift from God. God uses the ordinary things of our life to draw us into the extraordinary life of union with him.

The practice of reviewing our graces (counting our blessings) at the close of each day makes us more keenly attuned to the living presence of God in our lives. Equally important is praying for particular graces for ourselves and for others. This kind of prayer is like priming a pump. It starts the graces flowing into our lives.

Water is associated with daily chores: doing laundry, washing the car, sprinkling the lawn, to name a few. Many hours of our day are taken up with seemingly inconsequential activities. Seldom are we summoned to great acts of heroism. Few of us will do anything to change the course of history. That is why St. Therese of the Child Jesus so quickly won people's hearts. She showed us that sanctity is possible through little things. When someone splashed her with water or annoyed her by rattling rosary beads, Therese responded with silent endurance. When she experienced a natural dislike for a grumpy sister, Therese went out of her way to be nice to her. Her little way to heaven is reassuring.

Other holy people have shown us that humble work should not be scorned. Imagine how many trips to the well Mary made in her lifetime and how many meals Jesus prepared. When we carry out humdrum tasks well, especially when we do them for someone else, we are being saintly.

Water takes the shape of its container. To be life-giving to others, we have to fit ourselves to their needs. Like Paul, we are to strive to be all things to all people. To be the evangelizers we are called to be, we have to adapt to the young and the old, male and female, introvert and extrovert, conservative and liberal, the rich and the poor, the sick and the healthy, the Jehovah Witness, the unchurched, and the next-door neighbor.

The *Constitution on the Church in the Modern World* expresses it very well: "The joy and hope, the grief and anguish of the [people] of our time, especially of those who are poor or afflicted in any way are the joy and hope, the grief and the anguish of the followers of Christ as well.... Christians cherish a deep solidarity with the human race and its history" (n. 1). With prayer and practice we will be as adept as an actor or actress in assuming different roles. We will adapt our words, our approach, our actions, even our mannerisms and tone of voice to best relate to an individual to convey Christ's love.

Water teaches us that in unity there is strength. Of itself a droplet can do little either for good or for evil. But joined together in a waterfall, droplets can generate enough electricity to light a city. In an ocean, droplets can erode mountains. In a flood, they can destroy towns.

The community aspect of the church has always been vital. In the early days of the church, the first Christians lived a communal life and shared all things. Their unity caused observers to declare, "See how these Christians love one another." Today we see the rise of Christian communities and of support groups. More and more we are coming before the Creator as a people, gathering not only for the celebration of eucharist, but for Renew, Bible study, and healing services. Through the RCIA and service groups like the "Shepherds" of St. Noel Parish in Cleveland, parishes are recapturing the church's original spirit of cohesiveness. This tendency toward unity cannot but result in spiritual energy spilling over into the world as a positive force.

Giving a drink of water to someone thirsty is an elemental act of courtesy human beings perform for each other. Jesus accentuates this act when he says, "And I promise you that whoever gives a cup of cold water to one of these lowly ones because he is a disciple will not want for his reward" (*Matthew 10:42*). As a human being, Jesus himself sometimes needs a drink of water. Before he dies, one of the last things Jesus says from the cross is "I thirst." Implied in these words is a final request, not necessarily on the physical level. Who of us will quench the Master's thirst?

11

COIN

Let me see the money you pay the tax with. They handed him a denarius. Matthew 12:19

Jesus successfully evades a trap intended to lure him into uttering a treasonous statement. Rather than teaching that the Jewish people should not pay taxes, Jesus shrewdly replies that what is Caesar's should be given to Caesar and also what is God's should be given to God. To illustrate his lesson, Jesus holds in his hand a denarius, a silver coin. This coin was the tax tribute Rome demanded. It was equivalent to a day's wage.

The coin bore a graven image, the head of Caesar. Here was an idol on an idol, for both emperor and money have been worshiped in history. Men and women have been fascinated and duped by their power. Now the emperors are dead, but money still reigns.

In the Hebrew Scriptures, Joseph was sold by his brothers

for twenty silver coins. Jesus was sold for thirty silver coins. To-day many innocent men and women are treated in a similar fashion by their brothers and sisters in the human family. Greedy idolators use them to make money, exploiting them through evils such as unjust wages, fraud, pornography, and prostitution.

Much of Jesus' moral teaching has to do with our relation-ship with money and possessions. He exhorts us to have our treasure in heaven. He warns that it is difficult for a wealthy person to get into heaven. The heart of Jesus' message is that we are to share what we have. We are to love our neighbor, espe-cially the poor and the powerless, by meeting their needs, even if this entails sacrifice or surrendering some of our rights.

Some people view life as a game of Monopoly: whoever has the most money at the end wins. Logically this makes no sense because as an old saying puts it, "There are no pockets in shrouds." Nevertheless, there is some perverse drive within us that urges us to desire more and more, sometimes at other peo-ple's expense.

The Christian view of life as a cooperative venture has biblical roots. The people of God are a community working to-gether to establish a kingdom of peace, justice, and love. The kingdom is characterized by solidarity, partnership rather than competition, and it shows a special concern for the poor. Repeatedly Israel's prophets judged her according to her treat-ment of the widow, the orphan, and the stranger. Likewise Je-sus claimed that at the last judgment we will be saved or con-demned according to our treatment of the hungry, the thirsty, the stranger, the naked, and the imprisoned (*Matthew* 25).

However, it is very easy to be like the complacent man in the parable who lives in luxury, oblivious to Lazarus, the dying beggar on his doorstep. Every once in a while we need to have our eyes opened so that we realize what we are doing or neglecting to do. Otherwise after death we may find ourselves next to the rich man, eternally longing for a drop of water from the blessed in heaven.

By issuing the pastoral letter *Economic Justice for All,* the United States bishops have taken the role of the little boy in the fairy tale "The Emperor's New Clothes." In this tale all the citizens go along with the crowd in admiring the emperor's new clothes as he processes down the street. Then suddenly a boy declares the truth: the emperor isn't wearing anything! The pastoral letter proclaims some facts. Today 800 million people outside the United States live in absolute poverty, while 33 million Americans are poor. An estimated 28% of the total net wealth in the United States is held by the richest 2% of its families. Of the 17 industrialized nations in the Organization for Economic Cooperation and Development, the United States is almost last in percentage of gross national product devoted to foreign aid. The bishops also remind us of some Christian principles: all humans have dignity; people have a right to contribute to the community through work; and God is hidden in those most in need.

The letter raises hard questions: Does our economic system place more emphasis on maximizing profits than on meeting human needs and fostering human dignity? Aren't we diverting minds and money from bettering human life to projects that threaten death? Is it right to pressure poor countries to buy weapons when they need food, medicines, and education so badly? The recommendations of the letter are worth considering, especially the fundamental call to devote our creativity and commitment to solving economic problems for the sake of our families and for the sake of the future.

Jesus advises that we give to God what belongs to God. In reality, everything belongs to God. The church father St.

Cyprian taught that "whatever belongs to God belongs to all." Therefore, "misuse of the world's resources or appropriation of them by a minority of the world's population betrays the gift of creation" (*Economic Justice for All*, 34). The bishops state, "That so many people are poor in a nation as rich as ours is a social and moral scandal that we cannot ignore" (16).

Today we are asked to extend justice and charity not only to the person we find beaten and robbed on our own roads, but to the poor and oppressed all over the world. Advanced technology has made us a global village where the people on the other side of the world are our neighbors. All men, women, and children on our planet earth constitute the human family. How sad that while some members starve to death, others' chief concern is losing weight. We have an obligation to promote interdependence and to assist developing countries. If we care enough, we can help shape government policies that affect the quality of life here and abroad. As Christians we are called to be on the cutting edge of social reform. That's what "Thy kingdom come, Thy will be done on earth" is all about.

By law a percentage of our income goes to Caesar. But we are free to make donations to God (though pastors would be greatly relieved if the practice of tithing were revived). It might be revealing to work out what percentage of one's income is given to God. Another interesting exercise would be to imagine winning a million dollars in a lottery and to speculate how one would spend it.

Money is power. Those who have it in abundance can live like gods. Ironically, the true God, when becoming human, chose to shun both money and power (*Philippians 2:7-8*):

he...emptied himself
to assume the condition of a slave,
and became as men are
and being as all men are,

he was humbler yet,
even to accepting death,
death on a cross.

Jesus invites us, "Learn from me, for I am gentle and humble in heart" (*Matthew 11:29*). The weak and lowly know faith. Someday they will know the reward of faith. For in Mary's words, God "has exalted the lowly" (*Luke 1:52*).

Coins are minted and issued by governments as a medium of exchange. They have value because of their purchasing power. Everyone is born with certain gifts. Like coins, these natural gifts are worthwhile to the extent that they are used. To identify our gifts, to develop them, and to use them to advance the kingdom is our fulfillment and joy as human beings. Janet Stuart knew this: "Trade with the gifts God has given you." We must trade not only our skills and our talents, but our supernatural gifts, too. This is what Peter did. He said to the crippled beggar at the Temple entrance, "I have neither silver nor gold, but I will give you what I have: in the name of Jesus Christ the Nazarene, walk" (*Acts 3:6*). We may not have the power of healing, but perhaps we have a strong faith, an understanding heart, or spiritual insight that can be shared with others. Jesus instructed us, "The gift you have received, give as a gift" (*Matthew 10:8* NAB).

An analogy I once heard illumines the value of sharing gifts. In Palestine there are two bodies of water fed by the Jordan River. One is fresh and clean. Fish thrive in it and lush green foliage adorns its banks. Trees stretch out their branches over it, and their roots drink its waters. Children play along its shore. People build their houses near it; and birds, their nests. Jesus liked to preach and to pray where he could look across its blue expanse. All kinds of life are happier because of this sparkling silver sea.

The Jordan flows south from this sea into another sea. Here there are no splashing fish, fluttering leaves, singing birds, or laughing children. The air above it is heavy. People avoid this sea. No living thing can drink from it. The difference between the two seas is that the Sea of Galilee receives but does not keep the Jordan water. For every drop that flows into it another flows out. The other sea hoards what it receives. It gives nothing. It is called the Dead Sea.

Our dynamic, modern church has the means to prevent us from becoming Dead Seas. The expanded role of the laity and numerous new ministries offer ample opportunities to put our gifts at the service of others. If we want to serve badly enough, we will. We are ingenious when it comes to making time to do the things we want to do.

We have the custom of tossing coins into fountains and wells and making a wish. If we Christians are to make an impact on the world, if we are to transform it into God's kingdom, we have to do more than wishful thinking. We even have to do more than praying, though this, of course, helps. We have to wake up, roll up our sleeves, and get to work.

12

FISH

...go to the lake and cast a hook; take the first fish that bites, open its mouth and there you will find a shekel. *Matthew 17:27*

In order to pay the Temple tax, Jesus, no doubt with a twinkle in his eye, sends Peter to catch a fish. It is not unusual for fish to ingest odd trinkets. It is unusual that Jesus predicts that the first fish caught will contain a coin worth enough to pay the tax for Peter and himself. It is even more unusual that Jesus chooses this roundabout way to pay the tax. After all, he could have told Peter simply to look on the ground or in his coin purse and, *voila*, the coin would be there. But it makes for a more delightful story to have Peter the fisherman fish the tax money out of the lake.

This is not the first time a fish is put to a singular use in the Bible. Recall the story of Jonah, the runaway prophet. God called Jonah to preach to Nineveh, the capital city of the archenemy. Overcome with fear, Jonah sailed in the opposite direction. When he was thrown overboard, a great fish was summoned to swallow him and to spew him out on the shore. Jonah was not only saved but became an enormous success, thanks to the fish.

In the Book of Tobit, Tobias was washing his feet in the river when a great fish almost swallowed his foot. At the angel Raphael's bidding, the boy caught the fish. He was able to use its heart and liver to drive away the demon that had killed his wife's first seven husbands on their wedding night. Later Tobias used the fish's gall as an ointment to cure his father's cataracts.

The fish in the Bible clearly are saviors and healers. Coincidentally, the early Christians saw in fish a symbol of Jesus. *Ichthys (IxΘus)*, the Greek word for "fish," became an acronym for the phrase "Jesus Christ, Son of God, Savior." Fish were a reminder of the saving and healing acts of Jesus and his power over sin and death. Drawn on the sand with the toe of a sandal or traced with the finger, a fish was the secret sign that identified Christians during the persecutions. It is still a visible symbol today in religious art, from stained glass windows to stickers.

Besides supplying tax money, fish figured in Jesus' life in other miraculous ways. Each time people were led to a deeper understanding of who Jesus was. When the disciples returned empty netted after a night of fishing, Jesus directed them to a huge haul of fish. Another time, he multiplied bread and fish to feed a famished crowd. Fish is even associated with the greatest miracle of all. On the day of the resurrection, to prove to his disciples that he was not a ghost, Jesus ate a piece of grilled fish.

Scripture doesn't tell us whether or not Peter actually found the coin in the fish. It shouldn't surprise us if he did. Isn't it equally thrilling to learn that pearls are found in oysters? That starfish regenerate? And that the skeleton of a certain fish resembles Christ on the cross? Not only the ocean, but the whole world is full of wonders. Fortunate are those whose sense of wonder is alive. Like a child who sees everything with fresh eyes, they can marvel at a milkweed pod, a spiderweb, and a sunrise.

Jesus compared us to fish. He commanded his apostles to be fishers of people. In a parable he said that the kingdom of heaven is like a dragnet that takes in all kinds of things to be sorted by angels. Tertullian echoed this comparison when he wrote *On Baptism*: "We are little fish and like the *Ichthys* Jesus Christ, we are born in the water; we are not safe in any other way than by remaining in the water." Dom Helder Camara, Archbishop of Olinda and Recife in Brazil, meditated on this same metaphor in *A Thousand Reasons for Living* (8 February 1978):

Watching a marvellous film
about the ocean depths
I felt a huge desire
to help the fish
understand how lucky they are
to live immersed
in so much splendour.
Imagine then my thirst
to cry to men, my brothers,
that we live immersed—
coming and going,
swimming to and fro—
not in the oceans
but in God himself!

Our oceans, lakes, rivers, and ponds are home for a seemingly endless variety of fish: exotic phosphorescent fish in the pitch blackness of the ocean, graceful angel fish, strange-looking swordfish, and the newly discovered orange roughy. Each is unique, each is special. The fish that appear most drab can be the tastiest. Similarly, each of us is different from everyone else. We each have gifts and flaws. The more we realize this truth, the less susceptible we are to exaggerated pride in our own gifts and to jealousy of other's gifts.

Fish travel in schools. People living and working together cooperatively have an advantage over individuals. The strengths of one compensate for the weaknesses of others. Furthermore, in a team or a community, synergy comes into play. In other words, the effect of the whole is greater than the effect of the sum of the individual members. Special powers and advantages are present in a group. The Mystical Body of Christ is a group. Animated by the Spirit and striving to live Christ's way, the people of the church can be a tremendous force in the world. Much of the work of the theologian Teilhard de Chardin dealt with the end of time when humankind will be totally unified in Christ. Then, just as the many different sounds of instruments in an orchestra blend to create beautiful music, we sons and daughters of God will join our voices in one glorious hymn of praise to God forever.

Fish are silent creatures. They do not speak, and noiselessly they glide through the water. Anyone who wishes to catch a fish must also be very quiet. Silence has intrinsic value. It is conducive to thought and to prayer. The small, still voice of God speaking out of the eternal silence is most easily heard in silence. In our day and age when radios and televisions are always on, when outside traffic is continuous, and when even the time we are put on hold on the phone is filled with music, silence is a luxury. Precious moments of silence must be planned and guarded jealously.

When we manage to treat ourselves to quiet time, we promote well-being in ourselves. Periodically stepping out from the frantic pace of life and the noise of our daily activities safeguards mental health. Silence also fosters spiritual growth. It is the air our spirit breathes so that our spiritual life may thrive. Jesus used to steal away from his cohorts in the early hours of the morning to be alone in silence. If he needed this kind of atmosphere, surely we do.

The Christmas liturgy contains this Scripture passage: "When peaceful silence lay over all, and night had run the half of her swift course, down from the heavens, from the royal throne, leapt your all-powerful Word" (*Wisdom 18:14-15*). When our hearts are silent, we invite a second incarnation. In the calm of silence, the Word is free to become alive and active within us.

Fish is related to penance, another practice that makes us more Christ-like. For many years a fish marked the Fridays on our calendars as days of abstinence from meat. Although "no meat on Friday" is no longer mandatory, penance remains a staple in Christian life and always will be. However, it is one of those Christian values that is threatened by contemporary trends. The modern emphasis on caring for oneself, building one's self-concept, becoming assertive, and relaxing militates against the self-denial advocated by our spiritual fathers and mothers. It takes wisdom, and sometimes the guidance of another person, to travel the healthy middle course between self-abuse and self-obsession.

Jesus tantalizes us with an apparent contradiction: to find our true self we must deny our self. Therefore, anyone seriously pursuing holiness, a life of perfect love, is interested in developing self-control. Our tendency is to cater to our own needs and desires. If we had a recording of our thoughts, it would reveal that we are preoccupied with ourselves: "What does he think of me? She hurt my feelings. If I do that for him, will he do this for me? She's wasting my time. I would rather not do that." Our anger is usually roused because someone has disturbed our pleasure or contradicted us. Our faults and sins are the result of satisfying our own wills, which serve our ego. To relocate the center of our attention and devotion from ourselves to other people and God requires much exertion.

If we wish to be strong enough to root out our vices, if we wish to be expert at love, we must "exercise," not by jogging or pumping iron, but by saying no to ourselves. As with any exercise, we must start small and then build. Often we find little acts of self-denial rather difficult: curbing our taste for sweets and junk food, our habit of useless chatter, and our curiosity. If we can refrain from making a comment that will steal the show, if we can resist the urge to have a second cup of coffee, if we can stay home to be with another when we feel like going out, then we are making progress. Then we are following Jesus who said, "If a man wishes to come after me, he must deny his very self...." (*Matthew 16:24* NAB). Even graphically, when the I is crossed out with a line, a cross is formed: ✝.

Penance is inherent in the normal acts of living. We needn't look for extraordinary practices. Wearing a smile when we feel like soggy cereal is as uncomfortable as a hairshirt and as meritorious. So is listening to a bore, being patient with a computer breakdown, and using our work time well. Actually, there are some days when getting up out of bed and forcing ourselves to do what we know we must is tantamount to climbing the scaffold steps or entering the arena to face the lions. Life's built-in penances can be more painful and demand more of us than abstaining from meat, especially if we happen to like fish. (After all, Marc Connelly's play *Green Pastures* depicts heaven as an everlasting fish fry.)

Today the reputation of fish as health food has grown. It has long been extolled as brain food. Now recent studies indicate that this cholesterol-controlling food is also good for the heart. Jesus, too, is good for the head and the heart.

13

TOWEL

...he got up from the table, removed his outer garment and, taking a towel, wrapped it round his waist; he then poured water into a basin and began to wash the disciples' feet and to wipe them with the towel he was wearing.

John 13:4-5

The night before he died, Jesus demonstrated in a striking way what he meant by "love one another." At the name of Jesus all beings in the heavens, on earth and in the underworld should bend the knee (*Philippians 2:10*), yet, Jesus knelt before his creatures and washed their feet. Peter was right to resist. Washing feet was the job of a servant, not a friend—much less a God.

Then Jesus declared that his followers should do the same. Every Christian should be girded with a towel as an invisible habit. We should always be prepared to pitch in and do a job that needs to be done for another person, no matter how demeaning or demanding. This could be as easy (or as hard) as drying the dishes.

The towel is the symbol of servitude. Those who wear it no longer look for ways others can meet their needs, save them time, or bolster their ego. Instead, they are alert to ways they can show love. In fact, they try to guess what words and acts will bring pleasure to others. They exercise the ministry of surprises.

We know we have the reputation of being a servant if people frequently ask us for favors. They are not afraid of getting a "no" or a grudging "all right." We might even be the type that people take advantage of and "walk all over." In this age of independence, glorifying of self, and speaking up for one's rights, this kind of service may be interpreted as weakness. But I wonder how Jesus views it—he who gave up food, sleep, and, in the end, his very life to help others.

We can be sure Mary, the Mother of Jesus, often wielded a towel. She, the queen of heaven and earth, spent many hours drying dishes, sewing and laundering clothes, and preparing meals. The earthshaking day that God became flesh in her body, Mary did not pamper herself, though that would have been understandable. No, she went as quickly as she could to minister to her aged relative who was also pregnant. Mary's sensitivity to the needs of others resulted in Jesus' working his first sign. And after the crucifixion, it was Mary who nurtured the infant church, no doubt sharing the tasks of the other holy widows.

Jesus turned around our concept of authority figures. No longer are they to be on a pedestal, lording it over their subservient subjects, and waited on, hand and foot. Rather, the leaders in the kingdom of God walk among the people caring for their needs, enabling them to be holier and happier members of that kingdom. It's not merely for the sake of decoration that priests and deacons wear a stole. The word "stole" is derived from *stola*, which is Latin for towel. Even the highest leader of the church, Pope John Paul II, at his inaugural Mass prayed, "Make me a servant of your unique power, of your sweet power, of your power that knows no eventide; make me a servant of your servants."

A towel has pleasant connotations. Think of wrapping yourself in a luxurious turkish towel after a hot bath, lying in the sun on a beach towel, and being presented with thick, fluffy guest towels on a visit. Towels are associated with warmth, security, and love. This is what we are meant to offer one another through our acts of service. As a towel is used in the process of cleansing, we can help wash from others' lives what is ugly and evil. We can teach them truth and show them goodness. As a towel absorbs water, we can blot another person's fears and tears. This service can be rendered by caring enough to take time to listen to people who are hurting. As a towel can invigorate us and bring a healthy glow to our skin, we can bring life to others by giving them hope and loving them.

Jesus washed not only our feet, he washed the whole of us. He took our sin upon himself, and the world was cleansed. What the flood of Noah couldn't do, the blood of Jesus did. Through his death and resurrection, Jesus made all things new. He is still serving us, still washing us. In the waters of baptism, he takes away all stain of sin. When it sullies us again during the battle of life, in the sacrament of reconciliation he restores us to our pristine baptismal beauty.

Not only should we let Jesus serve us by celebrating the sacraments, but we should also cultivate the act of graciously allowing others to serve us. Paradoxically we serve others by letting them serve us. A stubborn self-sufficiency deprives other people of the joy of loving. So let's ask for help, accept offers of help, and seek opinions. These acts of dependency can require as much humility as it takes to wash someone's feet.

In Psalm 116:12 we ask, "What return can I make to Yahweh for all his goodness to me?" A legend discloses the answer. It is said that Anthony the Hermit posed a question one day to his young students. He asked, "When is the first moment of daybreak?" One follower answered, "Is it when we can discern the forest?" "No," said Anthony. "Is it when we can distinguish one tree from another?" ventured another. "No," Anthony replied. "Tell us," said a third. Then Anthony said, "The first moment of daybreak is when we see the face of Christ in the face of our neighbor."

What we do to one another, we do to Jesus. This is the message of *The Story of the Other Wise Man* by Henry van Dyke. Artaban was to accompany Caspar, Melchior, and Balthazar on a pilgrimage to the newborn king of Israel. He has sold everything to purchase a sapphire, a ruby, and a pearl as tribute. When he sees the new star, he begins his journey to meet the three wise men according to plan. He is delayed when he stops to revive a dying Hebrew, and the other Magi leave without him. He must sell his sapphire to buy provisions for his solitary journey. In Bethlehem a young mother who offers him hospitality tells about strangers from the East who visited Joseph and his family. That night when Herod's soldiers came to slaughter the children, Artaban gives the captain the ruby to save the woman's baby. He spends the rest of his life searching for the king among the poor and ministering to them. Finally, in Jerusalem Artaban hears of a man who is to be crucified for claiming to be king of the Jews. He intends to offer his pearl as ransom for his life. But then he meets a troop of soldiers dragging a girl to be sold as a slave. She pleads for his help, and he gives her the pearl. Suddenly there is an earthquake and a tile strikes Artaban on the head. Bending over the old man, whose face is suffused with joy, the girl hears a faint voice say to him, "Inasmuch as thou hast done it unto one of the least of these my brethren, thou hast done it unto me!" The other wise man had found his king.

When Jesus washed the feet of the apostles, his brothers, it is significant that Judas was among them.

14

THORNS

...the soldiers twisted some thorns into a crown and put it on his head.... John 19:2

The crown of thorns was an instrument of torture during Jesus' passion. It inflicted dual suffering: physical pain from the long, sharp thorns piercing his forehead and scalp, and mental anguish because it was used in mockery.

Thorns quite naturally symbolize suffering. The expression "a thorn in the side" refers to anything that gives continual pain. Like a rose that possesses both a beautiful flower and a thorny stem, life offers us good things and bad. The good things we accept without question. The bad we regard as the greatest mystery of life.

After leaving the bubble-chamber of childhood, we become ever more aware of evil and suffering in the world. We learn of atrocious crimes committed by human beings throughout history, and those that are perpetrated today in homes, on the streets, in the business world, and in government offices. We discover petty and malicious thoughts lurking in ourselves. We are touched by the suffering of acquaintances. We encounter personal calamities and failure. Just when we think things can't possibly get any worse, they do.

Daily we suffer little pricks like misunderstanding, criticism, or the beginning of a cold. Occasionally we experience a crisis, depression, or an accumulation of bad luck so severe that we might be tempted to end it all by running our car off the road into a tree.

No one is exempt from suffering. Even those people who always act as if they just won a lottery have their share of tragedies. Behind every pleasant mask is a person who has known sorrow and pain to some degree.

There is a story about a woman who complains to God about her particular cross. In a vision God transports her to a room stocked with crosses of diverse dimensions and styles. He lets her choose one for herself. The woman spies the tiniest and prettiest cross and says, "I'll take this one." And God answers, "That's the one you already have."

Rabbi Harold S. Kushner addressed the problem of suffering in his book, *When Bad Things Happen to Good People*. He proposed that suffering implies that either God is not all-good or not all-powerful. Rabbi Kushner and others who wade into this unfathomable mystery arrive at no satisfactory answer. They are all left standing with Job before God stuttering, "I have been holding forth on matters I cannot understand, on marvels beyond me and my knowledge" (*Job* 42:3).

It is Jesus who at least imparts meaning to suffering. He suffered out of love. (How wonderful must be the Father's love that would evoke such loving obedience.) By his suffering and death, Jesus vanquished evil. When we suffer out of love for

God and others, we resemble Christ in his redemptive acts. Our suffering, united to his, has the power to bring about goodness in the world. This is why praying the Morning Offering is a tradition in good standing. In it we offer our sufferings, among other things, for certain intentions.

Conceiving of God's suffering and dying for his creatures was beyond the scope of the human mind. The Hebrews anticipated only an earthly savior. Mythology told of gods coming to earth to help human beings. For instance, the Titan Prometheus gave people fire and then suffered for his compassionate gesture. But it took the divine mind to produce the idea of God's dying for his people. In Jesus, omnipotence became vulnerable. The Suffering Servant foretold in Isaiah is God himself.

Because he suffered, God understands our suffering. In God we can find comfort. Jesus specifically invites us to come to him when we are heavily burdened. C.S. Lewis captures God's sensitivity to our suffering in *The Magician's Nephew*, one of the Narnia tales. Digory, a little boy, is worried about his mother who is extremely ill. He tells Aslan, the lion who is the Christ-figure. As the boy talks, the huge lion's eyes fill with great, shining tears. But he does not help Digory just then. Only later, through the obedience and bravery of Digory, is the mother cured.

A popular modern parable speaks of God's concern for us in our suffering (author unknown):

One night a man had a dream. He was walking along the beach with the Lord. Across the sky flashed scenes from his life. In each scene he noticed two sets of footprints in the sand; one belonging to him, and the other to the Lord.

When the last scene of his life flashed before him, he looked back at the footprints in the sand. He noticed that many times along the path of his life there was only one set of footprints. He also noticed that it happened at the very lowest and saddest times in his life.

This really bothered him and he questioned the Lord about it. "Lord, you said that once I decided to follow you, you'd walk with me all the way. But I have noticed that during the most troublesome times in my life, there is only one set of footprints. I don't understand why when I needed you most, you would leave me."

The Lord replied, "My precious, precious child, I love you and I would never leave you. During your times of trial and suffering, when you see only one set of footprints, it was then that I carried you."

Perhaps because suffering is related to God, the closer we are to him, the more we experience it. This is borne out by an episode in the life of Teresa of Avila. While crossing a river, she nearly drowns. When she scolds God, he replies, "That's the way I treat my friends." Teresa retorts, "That is why you have so few." Scripture suggests in the Book of Tobit and the Book of Job that suffering is a trial of our faith and love. Those who are agreeable to God have to be tried through suffering.

If this is so, then we must try to meet suffering with faith and love...like St. Joseph. Bishop Richard Keating of Arlington, Virginia, once gave a Christmas homily on St. Joseph. He began by recounting how, as a child, he had helped his mother set up the manger scene in their home every year. Their set had belonged to his great-grandmother. With the passage of time, statues had to be replaced, so that only a few were original. Mrs. Keating would carefully unwrap each piece and place it. She always put Mary on one side of the manger and Joseph on the other because they didn't match. Then every year she would step back, arms akimbo, shake her head and declare, "Either Mary or Joseph has to go." And each year Joseph returned to the closet until the next year's brief appearance.

One year Richard ventured to ask, "Why is it Joseph who always has to go back?" Mrs. Keating replied, "Joseph will understand."

In reflecting on this, Bishop Keating queries, "Can't you hear Mary saying to Gabriel at the Annunciation, 'Joseph will understand'?" Over and over Joseph is counted on to understand. His marriage plans are drastically altered. Then when his pregnant wife is almost due, a decree compels them to travel to Bethlehem. His foster son is born in a stable. Later Herod seeks the child's life, and Joseph must flee to a foreign land with his wife and child. There, among strangers, he must make a new life for them. Finally, Joseph died when he could have spent more years enjoying life with Mary and Jesus and when he could have shared their suffering.

But *did* Joseph understand? Not really. God's will was as incomprehensible to him as it is to us. Trust goes beyond understanding. Because Joseph loved and trusted God, he could work through his sufferings as part of a wise, though puzzling, plan. Each time he faced a painful event, he knew that somehow the dimensions of that cross would bridge the chasm from time to eternity.

We believe that God allows suffering and, as a loving parent, draws good from it. Nature teaches that suffering can result in something good. It is during or after a storm that the beautiful, ethereal phenomenon of a rainbow appears. One must first be pricked or scratched a bit by thorns in order to pluck blackberries. Only after enduring labor pains does a woman give birth. Kierkegaard observed, "All coming into existence is a suffering." Life's strange mixture of good and bad can cause us to feel joy simultaneously with suffering.

Usually when we know that we are undergoing something for the sake of others, we sustain an inner peace and joy. Seven-year-old Billy learned a lesson on suffering at a parish picnic. He enthusiastically joined in the water balloon toss until a balloon burst against his stomach and drenched him. On the verge of tears, Billy ran to his dad. "Look at it this way," Dad advised, "you kept someone else from getting wet!"

The thorn in our life could well be something we don't like about ourselves, such as an inclination to gripe, our cowardliness, or fits of anger. Just when we think we are traveling along smoothly on cruise control, headed directly for heaven, one of our uglinesses appears and throws us off course. This lack of control is painful and humiliating. But our imperfection can be the very means God intends to use for our salvation. The eighteenth-century Jesuit, Jean-Pierre de Caussade, advised a nun, "Rejoice every time you discover a new imperfection." Rather than becoming disgusted with ourselves and frustrated when we fail to meet our expectations, we should assume that God says to us what he said to St. Paul: "My grace is sufficient for you" (2 *Corinthians 12:9*). Moreover, we should say with Paul, "It is when I am weak, that I am strong" (2 *Corinthians 12:10*). The less we depend on ourselves, the more we will rely on God to act in our lives, and the more we will abandon ourselves to God.

Those of us who have the gift of faith have the wherewithal to endure sufferings great and small. Unbelieving sufferers, for whom suffering is useless and inane, can take heart from the thought, "And this too will pass."

Although thorns could be a protection for plants, the prince in *The Little Prince* by Antoine de Saint Exupery learns that sheep can eat his rose despite her four thorns. He then reasons, "Flowers are weak creatures. They are naive. They reassure themselves as best they can. They believe that their thorns are terrible weapons." Some people have so many thorns that no one can ever get close to them. Their scowling faces, sharp words, quick movements, and harmful actions may be weapons of self-defense. Unfortunately, these weapons merely serve to scare people away and make the fearful defenders lonely fortresses. Lord, protect me from such overprotection.

The Roman soldiers feigned honoring Jesus as king when they crowned him with thorns and threw a cloak over his shoulders. Ironically, they were acting out a reality. Jesus was in fact their king. He won the title King of the Universe through his suffering, death, and resurrection. Jesus is forever identified with both the royalty and the suffering which the crown of thorns embodies. In a way it is fitting that this crown was the only thing he wore when he died.

15

STONE

They found that the stone had been rolled away from the
tomb. *Luke 24:2*

The morning of the resurrection those who went to the
rock-hewn tomb of the Lord found that the stone before the entrance had been rolled away. In Matthew's account, the women
saw an angel who rolled the stone away and then sat on it. In
any case, this large stone was a sign that Jesus had risen. He
had broken the bonds of death. Just as plant life amazingly
pushes up through the nooks and crannies of rocky crags, Jesus
burst forth from the tomb. The corpse in the cave had been
transformed into the fully alive and glorified Messiah. Matter
could not restrain him.

If that stone had not been rolled away, if there had been
no resurrection, we probably never would have heard of Jesus.
He would have passed into oblivion along with the millions of
other people who once walked our planet and died. His life and

his death would have been insignificant. As it is, the resurrection gave credibility to the Man and his message and infused the world with hope. Now we worship Jesus as God. And now we have reason to believe that death is not a cul-de-sac, the end of life, but the gateway to a new and happier existence. We have reason to believe in a love that is stronger than death.

A primary class was preparing to act out the resurrection story. One boy stated that he wanted to be the large rock. "Why do you want to be the rock?" inquired his teacher. "So I can let Jesus out," the child replied.

To let Jesus out. This is our life's goal. We want to free him to be alive in us so that his energy may pulsate through us. The rocks that block him may be boulders or heaps of pebbles, things like a stubborn will, pride, selfishness, ignorance, laziness, and other faults. By dint of dynamite or erosion we remove these rocks. Yahweh asks in Scripture, "Does not my Word burn like fire...is it not like a hammer shattering a rock?" (Jeremiah 23:29). God's Word is one tool that can demolish whatever lies between Jesus and us. Listening to Scripture, reading it, mulling over it, and praying over it can change us. Sometimes a passage we have heard a thousand times suddenly, with startling clarity, applies to us.

The life of St. Augustine demonstrates the potency of Scripture. For the first thirty-two years of his life Augustine was alienated from Jesus. To his mother's dismay, he led a dissolute life and followed the heretical Manichees. He lived with a woman and had a son by her. Then one day he heard a child's voice chant repeatedly, "Take it and read." He opened a Bible and read the first passage he saw (Romans 13:13-14): "Let us live decently as people do in the daytime: no drunken orgies, no promiscuity or licentiousness, and no wrangling or jealousy. Let your armour be the Lord Jesus Christ; forget about satisfying your bodies with all their cravings."

In one glorious flash the path to Jesus was cleared for Augustine. He reformed and became a bishop in Africa as well as a prolific writer and speaker for the faith. His famous saying expresses the essential discovery of his life: "Our hearts, O Lord, are restless until they rest in you."

Once Jesus is free to act in us, he is released in the world. Through us the power of his love can penetrate and heal hard places, wounded places, and decaying places. He can revitalize the earth. Psychotherapist Scott Peck points out that *evil* is the opposite of *live*. By reversing evil with Jesus' help, not only do we live ourselves, but we enable others to live.

With Jesus living in us, our accomplishments, all the good we do, can be traced to him. No need to be puffed up by our successes in preaching, teaching, counseling, or the spiritual life. All is grace. He does more than we can ask or imagine when we give him free rein. We can rely on him like a rock.

"Rock" was a favorite Hebrew epithet for God. In Psalm 18 we pray: "I take shelter in him, my rock" (*v. 2*). "Who else is God but Yahweh, who else a rock save our God?" (*v. 31*). "Blessed be my rock!" (*v. 46*).

How is God like a rock? Rock is heavy, massive, and hard. It stands for might and dependability. When we stand in a canyon before a huge wall of rock, rest on a slab of granite, or clamber over rocks pounded by ocean waves, we sense a quiet strength. Recently, an educational magazine recommended that a dish of pretty, smooth stones be available for angry and aggressive students to use. Rubbing one of these "serenity stones" restores peace.

This is God for us: the rock bottom of the universe. He is always there, steady and silent, inscrutable and invariable. He is the solid Spirit that supports all. He is the rock of ages.

Happy are those who have God as the rock of their life. These are the people who acknowledge their dependence on

God, make him their center of gravity, and look to him for help. They are upheld by the assurance of God's deep and lasting love for them. Their world may fall apart, yet they stand firm. People may turn against them, criticize them, threaten them, and attack them, yet they remain calm. Their plans and projects may disintegrate into nothing, but they do not despair. They are founded on something far greater than the evanescent cares of this temporary life on earth.

Jesus, too, is called a rock. Paul saw the rock that gushed forth water for the Hebrews in the desert as a symbol for Christ (1 Corinthians 10:4). He is our life. Nothing else really matters on this earth: not our sins, not John of the Cross, not the charismatic movement, not church controversies—only Jesus.

Jesus is the stone rejected by the builders which has become the cornerstone (Acts 4:11). The whole building of the new creation depends on him. He holds the church together. When Jesus delegated his authority to Simon, he made a play on words. He changed Simon's name to Peter, which means rock. He said, "You are Peter and on this rock I will build my church. And the gates of the underworld can never hold out against it" (Matthew 16:18). The qualities of rock that correspond to God's characteristics also mark his church: strength and dependability. Popes, heretics, saints, bishops, theologians, and persecutors come and go. The church remains.

The church is founded on rock as was the house in Christ's parable. The house built on sand collapsed under the onslaught of a storm, whereas the house founded on rock weathered the wind, the rains, and floodwaters. The house on rock is Jesus' image for those who hear the word of God and follow it. The church, each of us members, is strong and safe as long as we remain faithful to God, true to our baptismal promises.

This means that we, too, must become like rock. We must strive to be firm in our commitments and unyielding to temptations. Perseverance, determination, faithfulness, and loyalty are acknowledged and admired attributes of a person of integrity. In Homer's *Odyssey*, Penelope is extolled for waiting faithfully for many years for her husband's return. She told her suitors she would marry one of them when her knitting was finished. Then every night she unraveled what she had knit during the day. Thomas More, chancellor of England, is a champion to all who would be true to their word. He gave his life rather than be swayed by his king-friend from what was right.

To be faithful to a commitment for years, especially when that commitment entails hardship and trials, is a real achievement. Those who manage to keep their promises through all the kaleidoscopic changes of life are nothing less than heroic.

In Scripture we are called living stones. Some of us are igneous rock, formed spontaneously by the fire of the Spirit. Some are sedimentary rock, being formed through long years of layered material and pressure. Some of us are metamorphic, formed through a drastic change. We may be a diamond or other precious stone, marble, or conglomerate, but whatever we are, we are important. Each of us has something to impart to the church that no one else has. If we don't give it, the church will be the poorer for it. Together we make the church what it is.

Stones are smoothed and polished naturally by the force of crashing waves. This process can be accelerated by using a machine that shakes the stones together. After a few days they are ready to be set into jewelry and other decorations. Our rough edges are worn off by rubbing shoulders with one another. It is through the friction of personal relationships, through conflicts, hurtful truths, compromises, and reconciliations that we become polished gems. Jean Vanier in *Community and Growth* wisely observes, "While we were alone, we could believe we loved every one. Now that we are with others, we realize how incapable we are of loving, how much we deny life to others."

Those people (in particular) who rub us the wrong way can make us saints. They afford us the opportunity to grow in many virtues, above all, in love. We should thank God for their presence in our lives. C.S. Lewis revealed one of the best secrets for strained relationships: "When you are behaving as if you loved someone, you will presently come to love him."

Since the Stone Age, human beings have exploited the pragmatic side of rock. We've built buildings, walls, walks, and bridges out of stone and made stone tools and weapons. Rocks have served as paperweights, doorstops, and even as pets. The glory of rock, though, is achieved when a sculptor chisels it into a work of art. Michelangelo's David, Moses, and Pieta, for instance, are among humankind's most splendid treasures.

Throughout our years on earth, the Master Sculptor works on us. With infinite patience and consummate skill, God chips away at the rough, unfinished rock that hides us until our true shape emerges. Our Creator delicately hones the lineaments and polishes the features, bringing us to the perfection we are meant to reflect for his glory. When we are finished—just as in the Greek myth Galatea who was carved out of ivory and loved by Pygmalion, her maker, came to life—we will wake to supernatural life. The beginning of our transformation is foretold in Yahweh's promise to Israel: "I will remove the heart of stone from their bodies and give them a heart of flesh instead" (*Ezekiel 11:19*).

At Jesus' triumphal entry into Jerusalem, the Pharisees urged him to stop his disciples from honoring him and acclaiming him king. Jesus responded, "If they were to keep silence, I tell you the very stones would cry out" (*Luke 19:40* NAB). The stones do shout out his greatness, as does the entire cosmos. The universe is bathed in God. And we, his friends in whom he dwells, in freedom and full consciousness, cry out in love and adoration: "Praise and glory and wisdom and thanksgiving and honor and power and strength to our God for ever and ever. Amen" (*Revelation 7:12*).